THE HISTORY OF LANDMINES

THE HISTORY OF LANDMINES

MIKE CROLL

LEO COOPER

First published in Great Britain in 1998 by
LEO COOPER
an imprint of
Pen & Sword Books Ltd
47 Church Street
Barnsley S70 2AS

Copyright © Mike Croll, 1998

ISBN 0 85052 628 0

Typeset by SetSystems Ltd, Saffron Walden, Essex
Printed in the U.S.A.

R0179925406

Contents

Acknowledgements

I would like to thank the staff of the following libraries: the Royal Engineers Library at Chatham, the Imperial War Museum Library, Bovington Tank Museum Research Centre, the US Army Ordnance Museum Library, Boston Public Library (Massachusetts) and the Royal Military Academy Sandhurst Library: unthanked guardians of knowledge all.

I am indebted to the following for supplying photographs: the Royal Engineers, the Imperial War Museum, Bovington Tank Museum, Aardvark Clearmine Ltd and Nick Bateman. Thanks also to Lyn Haywood for providing the excellent drawings and to my editor Dr J. B. Poole. Many others provided material and moral support including Paul Jefferson, Antonia Willis, my parents Kevin and Sally, and the members of the MGM deminers' forum at network@mgm.org. A special thanks is extended to my wife Elizabeth who shared the ups and downs of life in the field and whose encouragement and enthusiasm sustained me throughout this project.

While I am feeling sentimental I would also like to acknowledge the staff of the many organizations that I met during my career in the murky world of mine clearance including: the Royal Engineers and especially 33 (EOD) Regiment, The HALO Trust, DSL, ICRC, SGS, MAG, NPA, HI, MGM, Gerbera, GPC, Minetech, Mechem, the Krohn Organization, Ebinger GmbH, the engineers and ordnance technicians of the American, the Australian, the New Zealand, the Kuwaiti and the French Army, and (with a couple of notable exceptions) the United Nations. My sincere thanks also go to John Watkinson, Colin Mitchell and Arlindo Novela.

In particular I would like to express my appreciation to the local deminers of Mozambique, Cambodia, Afghanistan and Bosnia whose unfailing good humour and sang-froid in the face of a dirty, boring and dangerous task was always inspirational.

Finally, I dedicate this book: 'To those who walk the talk'.

Introduction

Landmines may be concisely defined as mass-produced, victim operated, explosive traps. The etymology of the word mine is derived from the Latin *mina* – a vein of ore – and was originally applied to the excavation of minerals from the earth. The technique and the term were borrowed by military engineers who dug mines during sieges and packed them with explosives to cause the collapse of fortifications. This form of classical military mining falls outside the scope of this book, but the expression was close enough to apply to the process of burying victim-activated explosive charges and from around 1880 onwards the word landmine gained common usage.

The concise definition excludes booby traps by virtue of the term 'mass-produced', although in reality the difference between landmines and booby traps can be academic. 'Victim-operated' excludes remotely-detonated devices which are important members of the landmine family and are covered within these pages, but to insert the word 'usually' in the definition appeared clumsy. Modern landmines are explosive traps, but they trace their lineage from non-explosive predecessors such as the spikes and stakes that were employed by ancient armies.

In the tactical defensive context, the use of concealed spikes and stakes is almost identical to that of the contemporary landmine. The concept can be traced back 2,500 years making it one of the oldest weapon systems in existence. Indeed, the four-spiked caltrop has been employed from Roman times to the present day without modification.

Despite its considerable history, little has been recorded about the use of these weapons and the reasons for this are perhaps threefold. First, there has been consistent under-reporting of defensive battles. Secondly, landmines and their predecessors have relied on concealment for their effectiveness and have been regarded as something of a secret weapon, the details of which are not readily disseminated. Lastly, they are a trap set by the cunning and detonated by the imprudent. Neither of these traits is publicized by the military man who prizes gallantry not trickery. Even Viscount Montgomery, whose forces were both saved and savaged by landmines in the great battles of North Africa, neglected to mention landmines in his *History of Warfare*.

The military's distaste for this style of warfare was neatly expressed by the British officer Colonel J.M. Lambert writing in 1952,

> 'Minewarfare is an unpleasant business. It is foreign to our character to set traps cold bloodedly, or to kill a man a fortnight in arrears so to speak, when you yourself are out of harm's way; and most British soldiers who have experienced it will own a rooted dislike of mine warfare in principle and in practice. There is too, something faintly derogatory about becoming a casualty from a mine; as a weapon of war it lacks the distinction of a shell or bullet. If one has to lose a foot (or one's life) it seems more respectable somehow for it to be done by a shell rather than a mine.'

At best, the use of mines has been considered an unchivalrous, practical necessity; at worst, in General Sherman's words, 'Not war, but murder'.

Landmines are subtle and much misunderstood weapons. Traditionally they are a means of transforming the terrain to the defender's advantage, rather than providing a definitive barrier. They can inflict casualties but need to be covered by fire. They shape the attacker's posture, but do not define the outcome of battle. They provide economies in defence while imposing attrition on the attacker. They are laid without relish and contemplated with fear. They are simple to lay but remarkably difficult to remove. They are not activated unless an attacker advances but they do not recognize ceasefires. The employment of landmines is complex and synergistic.

This book traces the history of the landmine from its earliest beginnings to the present day. It outlines its employment in selected campaigns and describes the broad developments in both mine and countermine technology through the ages. It is not encyclopaedic, nor does it offer detailed technical descriptions, rather it aims to illuminate the story of the landmine that has been buried for so long.

With anti-personnel mines having attracted the attention of the media and humanitarian groups recently, it is difficult to toe the line between historical objectivity and political correctness. Inevitably history is subjective and having been both an Army officer and a humanitarian deminer, I approach the subject from an informed but opinionated position. Today it is impossible to cover this subject without reference to the humanitarian perspective and without having one's morals scrutinized. It certainly has not been my objective to glorify what is surely one of the most insidious weapons ever developed nor to condone the suffering of the many innocent people killed and injured by them.

Standing on the edge of a minefield at Phum Sophie in Cambodia in 1992 with the first Khmer demining team, I flicked through the British Army's 'Pam 6' – *The Detection and Clearance of Mines and Explosive Devices*. I suddenly became aware that the procedures outlined there were identical to those used at El Alamein some half century before. After updating the drills considerably, I started to develop an interest in the history of landmines but could find no book on the subject. In the following year, clearing minefields in Pousat Province, I discovered some caltrops and later found reference to them in a book on Roman history . . .

Note

Fuse and fuze are not interchangeable terms. The first is used for safety fuse, that is, gunpowder-filled cord; the second denotes a mechanism to activate a mine or a bomb.

Chapter 1

Spikes, Traps and
Early Landmines

Traps

In 52BC Julius Caesar campaigned in Gaul to suppress an uprising against Roman domination. At a critical stage of the campaign the Gallic leader Vercingetorix withdrew his army of 80,000 to the fortified town of Alesia. Caesar deployed his army of 70,000 around the town intending to starve the Gauls into submission or flight, rather than risk attacking. However, on hearing that the Gauls were raising a large army to relieve their besieged compatriots, Caesar was faced with a dilemma. He could either retreat, abandoning Gaul, or he could attempt to maintain the siege while surrounded himself. Caesar chose the more daring option.

Inside Alesia, Vercingetorix had sufficient food for thirty days, forty if he reduced rations and expelled the non-combatants from the town and asked the Romans to take them into slavery. This he did, but Caesar, concerned about his own food supplies, did not accept them and they were left to starve between the opposing armies. The Gauls outside Alesia had only a limited time in which to raise an army to lift the siege before Vercingetorix was starved out. Messengers travelled throughout Gaul imploring men to join the struggle.

Caesar's situation was equally desperate. He faced the possibility of Vercingetorix's sallying out of Alesia and of a relieving force attacking his rear simultaneously. Caesar therefore set about creating two defensive lines to meet each threat. The inner perimeter was 16km long and the outer 20.7km, creating a strip

1

about 650m wide from which to conduct his defence. Caesar has left us with a detailed account of his preparations:

> 'He dug two trenches of equal depth each fifteen feet wide and filled the inner one, where it crossed the low ground of the plain with water diverted from streams. Behind the trenches a pallisaded rampart twelve feet wide was erected, strengthened by a battlemented breastwork, with large forked branches projecting where it joined the rampart to hinder the enemy if they tried to climb over. Towers were placed at intervals of a hundred and thirty yards along the entire circuit of fortifications.'[1]

Upon seeing these preparations the Gauls tried many times to break out of Alesia and through the defences, launching furious attacks against them. Ever mindful of the approach of a relieving Gallic army and conscious of his own limited numbers of soldiers, Caesar decided to make the defences even stronger to 'render them defensible by a smaller force'. In other words, the size of the defending force was inversely proportional to the strength of the fortifications.

> 'Accordingly tree trunks or very stout boughs were cut and their tops stripped of bark and sharpened; they were the fixed in long trenches dug five foot deep, with their lower ends made fast to one another to prevent their being pulled up and the branches projecting. There were five rows in each trench, touching one another and interlaced, and anyone who went among them was likely to impale himself on the sharp points. The soldiers called them boundary posts.[2] In front of them, arranged in diagonal rows forming quincunxes, were pits three feet deep, tapering gradually towards the bottom, in which were imbedded smooth logs as thick as a man's thigh, with the ends sharpened and charred, and projecting only three inches above ground. To keeps the logs firmly in position, earth was thrown into the pits and trodden down to a depth of one foot, the rest of the cavity being filled with twigs and brush wood to hide the trap. These were planted in groups, each containing eight rows three feet apart, and were nicknamed lilies from their resemblance to that flower. In front of these again were blocks of wood a foot long

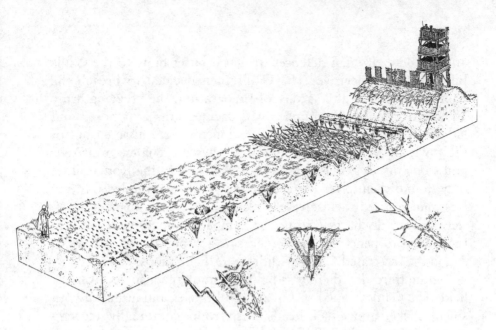

Caesar's field defences at Alesia. From left to right, *stimulus*, lilies and sharpened stakes.

with iron hooks fixed in them, called goads by the soldiers. These were sunk right in the ground and strewn thickly everywhere.'[3]

The depth of these defensive lines was roughly equal to the range of a strongly hurled spear, thus providing protection for the defenders while forcing the attackers to negotiate the obstacles under constant 'fire'. Additionally, Caesar left passages through the defences to enable his cavalry to ride against the attackers should the situation demand it.

The preparation of the defences took thirty days, by which time the situation for Vercingetorix was getting desperate, food was running low and there was no sign of a relieving army. A council held inside Alesia debated whether to capitulate or attempt a mass break-out. While they debated, a relieving force of 250,000 appeared over the crest of a nearby hill and the scene was set for one of the most remarkable of battles.

On the first day the Roman cavalry defeated the numerically-superior Gallic cavalry in an action in between the relieving force and the outer Roman defences. It was a bitter blow to the Gauls but it was not decisive. The Gauls then decided to breach the Roman lines and, after a day of preparation, the relieving army advanced at midnight equipped with facines, grappling hooks and ladders. On hearing the assault Vercingetorix led his men out of the town and into battle. There was a fierce exchange of arrows and stone missiles, but as the Gauls got close to the Roman lines they 'found themselves pierced by the goads or tumbled into the pits and impaled themselves, whilst others were killed by heavy siege spears discharged from the ramparts and towers . . . and they failed to penetrate the defences at any point', wrote Caesar. Again the frustrated Gauls withdrew to their camps.

On the third day there was fighting simultaneously all over the field. The Gauls heaped soil over the obstacles and attacked with shields locked above their heads, fresh troops continually relieving those who were tired. The hard-pressed Romans fought desperately, with Caesar redistributing his forces to meet each new attack. As the Gallic attacks were ground down on the defences, the Roman cavalry galloped through a series of 'safe lanes' and appeared suddenly behind them. The Gauls attempted to flee but, caught with no line of retreat, they were mown down. When the Gauls in the town saw their countrymen in flight they surrendered their arms and victory was Caesar's. He had won a great victory over a force five times as large as his own. Furthermore, he also demonstrated the value of traps and the Clausewitzian tenet that defence is the stronger form of combat.

From Caesar's use of goads, lilies and abatis one can trace the lineage of modern landmine warfare. Contemporary defensive minefields employ identical principles to the lilyfields of Alesia. Concealment causes the enemy to stumble unwittingly into a minefield without prior planning. Depth increases the time and resources required to clear a breach and provides a buffer zone for defenders who may remain out of range of attacking weapons. A variety of obstacles or mines forces an enemy to employ a range of clearance methods. Covering with fire creates a lethal distraction for an enemy attempting to clear obstacles. Safe lanes enable defenders to launch attacks on an attacker's vulnerable flank. The use of traps at Alesia allowed Caesar to wear down a numerically-superior army before it was crushed by cavalry. Throughout history landmines have been used as a force multiplier, boosting defensive strength beyond numerical strength.

The employment of concealed traps, or their explosive successors, on the scale of Alesia was not seen again until the North African campaigns of the Second World War. However, the limited use of similar devices has been a feature of warfare throughout the ages. In fact, the use of concealed traps to pierce the poorly shod feet of attacking soldiers or the hooves of horses had been practised for at least half a century before the siege of Alesia. Similar devices known as caltrops fashioned from bone were excavated from the Crimea and dated from the fifth century BC and other examples from India were employed to defend against elephant-mounted armies as early as the fourth century BC and Alexander the Great is reported to have used them during his great campaigns in the third century BC.[4]

Caltrops comprise four spikes, usually made of iron, joined at the centre and arranged so that when thrown on the ground, one spike always points upwards with the other three forming the base. One may imagine the efficiency of concealed caltrops. Massed ranks of soldiers rushing towards an enemy, skewering their feet on unseen spikes, falling over and suffering further wounds from other caltrops hidden in the grass, while the enemy launches spears at the wounded and prostrate bodies. An attack would rapidly turn into disarray, the front ranks being pressed forward by the rear who would not see what was happening ahead of them in the tightly packed formations of the pre-gunpowder age.

Quick to assimilate military technology, the Romans seem to have made regular use of caltrops in defence. Perhaps not anticipating their use during what they expected to be offensive campaigns in Gaul, they were forced to improvise the less versatile goads. It seems probable that a supply of caltrops was kept available for use in their Roman forts[5] and Procopius reports that they were strewn in front of open gateways during the siege of Rome.[6] Herodian also records their use by the Romans in open battle:

'And when the size of the cavalry and the number of camel began to cause them [the Romans] trouble, they pretended to retreat and then threw down caltrops and other iron devices with sharp spikes sticking out of them. They were fatal to the cavalry and the camel riders as they lay hidden in the sand, and were not seen by them. The horses and the camels trod on them and (this applied particularly to the camels with their tender pads) fell on to their knees and were lamed, throwing the riders off their backs.'[7]

The use of caltrops probably died out during the Dark Ages but was revived during the Renaissance.

During the English Wars of the Roses (1455–85) the development of the caltrop advanced a stage with an innovation in the form of nets about 24ft long and 4ft wide with a nail standing upright at every second knot.[8] The use of such nets must have been highly effective, enabling rapid emplacement and repositioning, but no other record of their use has been found. The utility of caltrops did not escape the fertile and practical mind of Leonardo da Vinci (1452–1519) who also recommended a countermeasure. He advised cavalry forces that caltrops should be carried behind the saddle in a leather bag and, if pursued, 'you should scatter them behind you. But should you have to cover the ground again it is advisable to be prepared and shoe your horses with an iron plate between the hoof and the shoe.'[9]

The use of caltrops appears to have been widespread from the fifteenth century onwards with examples of their use recorded in many European countries and even by early settlers in Virginia as a defence against Indians. The lowly caltrop also finds its place in twentieth-century military inventories from south-east Asia[10] to Northern Ireland, where the British Army link them with chains and use them to pierce the tyres of cars that speed through roadblocks. (The author discovered caltrops of an almost identical design to those used by the Romans in Cambodia in 1991.) Even the latest James Bond film 'Tomorrow Never Dies' has the hero scattering caltrops to puncture the tyres of the pursuing villain's vehicle.

The demand for military equipment to be 'soldier-proof' (i.e., both reliable and simple) has ensured the durability of the caltrop. With a design almost unchanged in 2,500 years, they may be the longest serving piece of military hardware in existence. However, a warning of their residual effect (and that of the landmine) was sounded by Francis Markan writing in 1622, 'the foards are soon choakt up with calthorpes' thereby rendering them impassable for men, horses and cattle long after hostilities had ceased.[11]

The Roman style 'lily pits' continued to be employed by infantry facing cavalry for many hundreds of years. Gregory of Tours, who died in AD593, alleged that the Thuringians used them against King Theuderic's army:

'They dug ditches in the future field of battle, and covered them over closely with sods, so that they seemed part of the unbroken plain. When the encounters began, numbers of Frankish horsemen fell into these ditches and were sorely hindered; though when the trick was discovered they began to look more cautiously about them.'[12]

The tactic was employed most famously by the Scots at the Battle of Bannockburn in 1314. The Scots, concerned about their exposed flanks and the possibility that English cavalry would break their ranks, made effective use of concealed defences. They dug pits 'a foot across, the depth of a man's knee and as thickly set as cells in a honeycomb . . . and concealed with grass laid on sticks.' In addition, they scattered caltrops about the field and disrupted the unsuspecting English cavalry charge.[13] Learning from the experience, the English used the same tactic against the French at Crécy thirty-two years later. The same practice continued to be employed as late as 1914 when the Germans dug similar pits known as 'wolf holes' in the battlefield of Ypres.

It should be noted that in nineteenth-century Europe concealed mantraps were used by landowners to catch poachers and trespassers. These generally consisted of a pair of hinged jaws that closed about the victim's leg when he stepped on a central, tilting plate. The mantrap was capable of lacerating flesh and crushing bone, but the principle objective was to restrain a poacher until he could be apprehended. These devices do not appear to have been employed in a military setting as they were expensive, heavy and difficult to conceal.

While the modern landmine can trace its heritage in both

tactical usage and design function to ancient forms of trap, the concealed spike was to have a renaissance in the jungles of Vietnam. The Vietcong improvised a wide variety of traps and spikes for use against American infantrymen. The most notorious design was the *panji* stick, a camouflaged pit containing sharpened and often poisoned bamboo sticks. The unwary infantryman would stumble into the pit, impaling his feet on the spike in a similar fashion to the Gauls at Alesia. The Vietcong, however, normally used their traps as booby traps, often along jungle paths, rather than as static defences. Their effectiveness was manifest in American medical statistics which indicate that 2 per cent of American casualties were caused as a result of men stepping on spikes or traps.

The Fougasse

It was inevitable that gunpowder would eventually be used in concealed weapons, both victim- and command-initiated. Gunpowder was used in China by the twelfth century and by the thirteenth it was employed in a form of landmine known as the 'underground sky soaring thunder'. This consisted of a small group of lances, pikes, flags or other attractive objects set in the ground to attract trophy-collecting enemy horsemen. The act of pulling a pole from the ground initiated an igniter attached to a buried gunpowder charge.[14]

The discovery of gunpowder in Europe is often attributed to the English Franciscan friar Roger Bacon (1214–92) who restricted knowledge of it. However, by the fourteenth century, gunpowder was in military use and its composition and manufacture were gradually improved over the next few centuries. The introduction of gunpowder must have had a profound effect on medieval man; the historian Polydore Virgil wrote in 1499 that 'of all other weapons that were devised to the destruction of man the gones [guns] be the most devilische.'[15] Despite the general distaste for gunpowder, the spirit of the Renaissance ensured its proliferation and technical improvement. By 1530 experiments had been conducted in the use of landmines in Sicily and southern Italy.[16]

These earliest gunpowder landmines are more correctly termed fougasses – essentially an underground cannon, placed forward of a defensive position to shower rocks and debris over a wide area. However, unlike a cannon, once fired they could not be reloaded and their employment was limited to a few vulnerable areas where they were fired as a last, desperate measure. Once the principle of the fougasse had been established its design remained virtually unchanged through to the twentieth century.

It is likely that the fougasse was a regular but minor feature of a defensive posture for centuries. It was rarely decisive and frequently unreliable. It had the potential to stop a massed attack but it was always peripheral to the main weapon systems and the stoical efforts of defenders. The capricious reliability of the fougasse stems from two serious limitations. First, gunpowder is hygroscopic which means that it absorbs water from the air and therefore looses its explosive ability. Without adequate water-proof containers early fougasses could be emplaced only a few hours or days before an attack, which could often be difficult to predict. Secondly, until William Bickford invented the safety fuse in 1831, powder trains had to be poured across ground exposed to rain, wind and atmospheric moisture. Therefore defenders lighting the fuse could never be certain whether their efforts would literally fizzle out.

Despite early technical limitations, fougasses, the 'poor man's artillery', were used to supplement defences on occasions. At the request of the Council of Malta, Francesco Maradon demonstrated the firepower of the fougasse in 1740. The Council was so impressed that it established a network around the coast and by 1770 over fifty operational systems were in place overlooking possible landing sites.[17] The remains of fougasse chambers may still be seen on Malta; the best preserved are at Selina.[18] In September 1846 at the siege of Chapultec, five miles south-west of Mexico City, the Mexicans dug fougasses 'amongst the vertical approaches, though the Americans managed to cut most of the fuzes' before they were fired.[19]

Related in concept to the fougasse was the spring gun. This was used in England from about 1800 until 1830 when, presumably because of its lethal and potentially indiscriminate effect, it was made illegal. Like the mantrap, the spring gun was a civilian device for use against poachers. It consisted of a short gun, loaded with shot and mounted on a vertical swivel. The gun was attached to two wires which when moved would 'swing' the gun in the direction of the intruder and fire the shot. Like the mantrap it had only limited military applications. Although it had the potential to kill an intruder, it lacked the marksmanship of a rifleman or the firepower of the fougasse. In the 1960s a device similar in concept, known as the SM-70, was deployed along the East German border.

The development of electrical initiation systems in the second half of the nineteenth century greatly improved the utility of the fougasse by allowing reliable, instant firing. Although high explosives were also developed during this time (nitroglycerine in 1847 and dynamite in 1866), gunpowder, a low explosive with an efficient 'heave' effect, was still generally preferred for fougasses. The use of the electrically-initiated fougasse (and sea mines) was pioneered by the Russians who used electrical initiation during the seige of Silistria during the Russo-Turkish War of 1828–29, but the technology was not disseminated. The technology was developed, apparently independently, during the American Civil War of 1861–65 with more enduring results.

The American Civil War formed the cusp between old style and modern wars. It was a bloody affair in which the stoicism of the American farmboy was thrown in close order against the mass-produced weapons of the fledgling industrial age. Although the Americans had no experience of general war before 1861, both sides rapidly mobilized huge armies and made many advances in military technology. The fougasse (and, as we shall see, the pressure-operated landmine) was largely a Confederate weapon and was used in many defensive actions. The proliferation of fougasses and other types of landmine was a result of early success in the use of mines against Union ships on the Mississippi, the Potomac and along the Atlantic coast. By the end of the war, landmines (or torpedoes as both land and water mines were termed during the period) had sunk twenty-nine and damaged fourteen Union ships; a greater tally than all the warships of the Confederate Navy.[20] The ability of a cheap mine to destroy an expensive warship was an irresistible economic argument for its employment.

10

Matthew Fontaine Maury demonstrated the possibilities of the electrically-initiated floating mine to the Confederate Secretary of the Navy in June 1861. Setting his mine in the James River, Virginia he initiated it 'using a spark passed through a long insulated cable' and 'up went a column of water fifteen or twenty feet' causing 'many stunned or dead fish', wrote his son who was present. Maury was immediately given the rank of captain and provided with $50,000 to refine his contraption.[21]

The first success of electric floating mines was on the Yazoo River, a tributary of the Mississippi, on 12 December 1862. The USS *Cairo* sank within minutes of two mines being detonated on her port side by a Confederate firing party including a Lieutenant Isaac N. Brown, CSN. Brown reported that he was torn by conflicting emotions when the *Cairo* sank, 'much as a schoolboy . . . whose practical joke has taken a more serious turn than expected'.[22]

Brown earns his place in the history books not only for being the first person to sink a ship by use of mines: together with Maury he planted what were probably the world's first operational electrically-fired landmines at Randolph Bluff above Columbus, Kentucky on the Mississippi during the summer of 1861. The landmines had squat iron casings with handles resembling cooking pots. Inside the landmines were 4lb artillery shells filled with canister and grapeshot; they were planted in clusters and rigged to be initiated from a nearby cave.[23]

In fact, the position at Columbus was abandoned without any mines being fired. In March 1862 advancing Union troops, forewarned by deserters of their presence, located scores of mines after investigating areas of disturbed soil. They were described in *Harper's Weekly* of 29 March 1862 as 'infernal machines' with which 'whole regiments could be blown up and sent to eternity, without even a chance of escape.' The magazine includes two etchings; one of a landmine complete with electrical firing mechanism and another of soldiers using shovels to excavate the mines.[24]

The heavily outnumbered Confederates experimented with fougasse-style mines throughout the war in an attempt to produce a means of addressing the imbalance between the armies. One new design featured:

'A steel tank, 4 feet long by 3 feet broad, and 10 inches deep, was used to hold scrap iron. The receptacle for the charge was a case of sheet iron with a very heavy base, and a strong cap of cast iron connected together by a stout spindle. When the charge exploded, the light sides of the case were blown out, and the top, which was retained in its place by the spindle and the base, gave a nearly horizontal direction to the contents of the tank. This kind of mine was never put into operation as the Federals never approached it: but from an experiment conducted in the woods near Petersburgh, where screens were erected to represent troops advancing near the site of the mine, the effect must be very great.'[25]

The exact date is not specified, but this must rank as one of the earliest scientific experiments of fragmentation mines ever conducted. Although there is no recorded evidence of their effect in combat, they must have been devastating, sweeping scythelike through ranks of infantry in the open. The economy they provided for the defender and the prudence instilled in the attacker are apparent from the following passage:

'The Confederate [en]trenchments of Petersburgh on the left were, during the latter operations of the war, provided with them [fougasse mines], and such was the protection they afforded that only two companies per mile were sometimes left to hold the works rear of these torpedoes . . . Elsewhere dummy mines were frequently established . . . the fact that such mines were never passed over by an assaulting column proved that they did their work.'[26]

Union troops were later to discover that an artillery bombardment on a suspected minefield could cut electrical cables and disrupt the mines. This procedure, while generally effective, also added to the burden imposed by mines. More ammunition would have to be manufactured, transported and fired, and the ground assaulted would take more time to cross, having been churned up by a thorough bombardment. Thus the increase in time and resources imposed upon the attacker by landmines greatly multiplied their effectiveness.

Despite the knowledge of more lethal devices, British military engineering books issued until the 1930s retained descriptions of the stone fougasse that had remained largely unchanged in 300 years:

'Fougasses should, as a rule, be fired by observation only. Their moral effect is considerable, and they may be especially useful against troops attacking on a narrow front. For a stone fougasse an excavation is made in the form of a cone or pyramid, a box of powder is placed in a recess at the bottom, and on the box a wooden platform or shield 3 or 4 inches thick, over which stones, etc. are piled . . . Fougasse may be fired by electricity or by hose and fuse . . . A fougasse of the form shown [see diagram], charged with 80 lb of powder should throw 5 tons of bricks and stones over a surface about 160 yards long and 60 yards on either side of the axis . . . with a charge of 30 lb of powder and ¾ ton of flints or stones it has covered by its explosion a space in its front of about 200 yards long and 90 yards wide . . . In easy soil two untrained men can dig out a fougasse in 8 hours.'[27]

The fact that the British Army was able to state charge weights and ranges of the fougasse confidently suggests that they were familiar with their use. They had little hesitation in using them during their colonial expeditions such as the Sudanese campaigns of 1884–88 and during the Boer War of 1899–1902. In Sudan the benefits of using electrical mines ensured that 'the mined ground would be forbidden to the enemy for his attack, but would not be forbidden to the defenders for any counterattack which it might be desirable to make'.[28] During the Boer War, while defending Ladysmith, 'seven electrical minefields were established [by the British] and some sixty mines laid . . . there was however, no opportunity of firing any pattern in earnest.'[29]

Doubtless the fougasse played a minor role in many actions but they lacked the necessary flexibility and reliability to be of great value except in static defence and they took considerable time to prepare. Unlike other weapons, once deployed they could not be moved to engage an enemy, although their deterrent effect may have been sufficient to justify the effort in constructing them. The

13

refinement of the machine-gun and improvements in artillery relegated the fougasse to something of an impracticable oddity by the start of the First World War. Curiously, during the Muslim–Croat conflict in central Bosnia (1991–93), where limited military hardware was available, combatants were forced to improvise weapons. Among the most remarkable was the use by Croats of a huge catapult to hurl water boilers full of explosive into the Muslim-held Vitez pocket. Furthermore, the fougasse was revived by both sides in central Bosnia in 1993.[30]

In the mid-1950s the concept of the fougasse was reborn in the guise of the pocket-sized, reliable and extremely lethal American M18A1 anti-personnel directional fragmentation mine, better known as the 'claymore'. The claymore contains 1,600 steel balls fixed in front of 1.5lb of high explosive in a plastic case. It can be set up in a few minutes and is initiated electrically, spraying its steel balls out to a lethal range of 50m. Its tactical employment is identical to that of its predecessor the fougasse.

Early Pressure Mines

Pressure-operated landmines are deployed in a similar fashion to ancient forms of trap and spike. They may be used *en masse* to create or enhance defensive positions, or individually to inflict casualties and induce caution. By using explosives rather than spikes, landmines are capable of producing far more devastating effects on the human body and, unlike spikes, the wounds they inflict are not proportional to the weight acting upon them. The pressure-operated landmine can be designed to function in response to a pressure of a few pounds and its effects, depending upon the quantity of explosive used, may range from amputation of the foot to the obliteration of the body. Its psychological effect is therefore considerably greater than that of the caltrop or the fougasse.

The technology to build crude forms of this type of landmine has been available since the sixteenth century. Early experiments with these devices would have shown them to be even less reliable than the fougasse and much more expensive than the caltrop. The concept of the pressure-operated landmine therefore remained on the drawing board for perhaps three centuries. The earliest description of such a mine is provided by the German military historian H. Frieherr von Flemming. In his book *Der Vollkomme Deutsche Soldat* ('The Perfect German Soldier'), 1726, Flemming describes how to use a *fladdermine* (literally flying mine). It consisted of a ceramic container with glass and metal fragments embedded in the clay containing 2lb of gunpowder, buried at a shallow depth in the glacis of a fortress and actuated by someone stepping on it or touching a low-strung wire.[31] The containers were manufactured in the Dutch town of Heerlen and exported to many parts of Europe. The glacis of a well-defended, star-shaped fort of the gunpowder age would have been sufficiently hazardous for an attacker without the introduction of the *fladdermine* and no accounts of their use in battle exist. It was not until the second half of the nineteenth century that pressure-operated mines became a regular feature of warfare.

It was the American Civil War, through a combination of factors, that precipitated the introduction of these mines. It was essentially a mobile war with defensive actions fought behind hastily constructed positions based, where possible, on natural obstacles. In the face of a superior enemy the Confederates needed to enhance their defensive lines to ensure that Union troops were exposed to as much attrition as possible. Additionally, victim-operated mines could cover a withdrawal without the need to sacrifice troops in rearguard actions. Thus the demand for land-mines coincided with a period in which technology was sufficiently advanced to fulfil it. Although lacking the range and mass destructive power of the fougasse, the pressure-operated landmine had several advantages: it was easier to conceal, less susceptible to artillery disruption and did not require a firing party. Also, although the significance was not fully appreciated at the time, the new weapon produced a caution in attackers, hitherto unknown.

It was perhaps inevitable that the inventive ability of the Americans, with their fascination for automation, would produce a weapon that would kill its victim without the need for a trigger to be pulled. Although the vague concept of pressure-operated landmines had been mentioned for many years in Europe, it is unlikely that the American citizen-soldier was aware of them. It is therefore reasonable to credit (or reproach) the Americans with the development of the first operational devices.

The invention and initial use of these mines is attributed to Brigadier-General Gabriel J. Rains of the Confederate States Army. As early as 1840 Rains had experimented with explosive booby traps while leading military units against Indians in Florida. His experiments had only mixed success but the idea was to remain with him. In the spring of 1862, commanding a garrison of 2,500 men at Yorktown and faced by General McClellan's Union Army of 100,000, Rains ordered his troops to prepare artillery shells so that they could be exploded by pulling trip wires or by being stepped on. These were buried around the fortifications, in the town and on the approach roads. In what was to become a common minelaying tactic, about 10ft from each device on the defender's side, a small flag was planted to warn friendly forces of the concealed hazard.[32]

On 4 May 1862, while scouting along a road leading to Yorktown, a horse from a detachment of Union cavalry activated a landmine, falling dead and leaving the rider injured. Later the same day one Union soldier was killed and three others were wounded by a landmine close to the Confederate lines. The pressure-operated landmine had claimed its first victims. That same night the Confederates slipped out of Yorktown and made for Richmond, pursued by Union troops. Slowed by mud on the road, Rains ordered more mines to be buried behind them, 'mainly to have a moral effect in checking the advance of the enemy and . . . to save our sick', he later explained. After setting off several of the mines, the Union cavalry hesitated, leaving Rains and his men to reach Richmond in safety.

The use of landmines caused serious discussions on both sides. Some of the Confederate enlisted men thought them 'barbaric' and General James Longstreet, Rains's commanding officer forbade their further use, declaring them neither a 'proper nor effective method of war'. The debate raged on, reaching the Southern Secretary of War George W. Randolph, who vindicated Rains by stating that landmines could be employed in roads to delay pursuit, in front of defences to repel attack, and in rivers and harbours to attack warships. Longstreet remained unconvinced and in a tactful manoeuvre Rains was assigned to work on the defences of the James and the Appomattox River where the use of mines would not be questioned.

Meanwhile, back in Yorktown Union troops were trying to come to terms with the unseen enemy. Charles A. Phillips of the 5th Massachusetts Battery of Artillery wrote, 'A blood stain on the ground where a man was blown up . . . and a little red flag ten feet from it admonishes to be careful. The rebels have shown great ingenuity . . . for our especial benefit.'

An outraged McClellan telegraphed his superiors:

'the rebels have been guilty of the most murderous and barbarous conduct in placing torpedoes within abandoned works near wells and springs; near flagstaffs, magazines, telegraph offices, in carpet bags, barrels of flour, etc. . . . I shall make the prisoners remove them at their own peril.'[33]

The situation was not as serious as McClellan suggested. Only a few devices exploded and perhaps three dozen men were killed or injured.[34] The psychological damage was sufficient though; soldiers would have imagined every conceivable place to be booby- trapped. An atmosphere of fear would have pervaded the abandoned Yorktown and all other places subsequently attacked and occupied by Union troops.

During winter of 1862–63 Rains worked at designing a primer designed to 'explode from the slightest pressure'. After losing the forefinger and thumb of his right hand, he decided to settle for a pressure of 7lb. The exact composition of the fuze remained a close secret during the war but the formula, revealed later, consisted of 50 per cent potassium chlorate, 30 per cent sulphuret (sulphide) of antimony and 20 per cent pulverized glass. The mixture ignited when a thin copper cap was crushed, this in turn lit a short fuse exploding the powder.[35] The 'Rains fuze' was normally set on top of a 7- or 8-in spherical artillery shell and, when activated, would have been lethal to the victim and dangerous to a radius of 30m and more. Rains was provided with a budget of $20,000 for his work with 'torpedoes' during 1863 and it appears that they were widely and successfully used throughout that period. Delighted with his work, the Confederate government assigned him to 'superintending of all duties of torpedoes' in 1864 with a budget of $350,000.[36]

As the Union Army under General William T. Sherman advanced on the Confederates' western flank many landmines were encountered. Sherman operated a savage scorched earth policy, burning buildings and destroying crops as he went. The Confederates therefore had little compunction in using mines both to slow the relentless Union advance and to kill soldiers ruining their land. At Fort McAllister, near Savannah, landmines killed twelve men and wounded eighty during the Union assault. After the battle Sherman claimed that 'it was not war, but murder' and put prisoners to work clearing the devices, despite the complaints of the Confederate commander Major George W. Anderson who claimed that 'this hazardous duty' was 'an unwarrantable and improper treatment' of his men.[37] The pragmatic Sherman eventually resigned himself somewhat to the use of landmines stating, 'I now decide the torpedo is justifiable in war in advance of an enemy. But after the adversary has gained the country by fair warlike means . . . the case entirely changes. The use of torpedoes in blowing up our cars and the road after they are in our possession, is simply malicious. It cannot alter the great problem, but simply makes trouble.'[38]

A few thousand landmines were planted around the approaches to Richmond, with Rains[39] personally supervising the placement of 1,298 during the fall of 1864. Each mine was marked with the small, red, warning flag and white tapes marked safe lanes for Confederate troops.[40] It was noted that by the end of the war 'the establishment of little red flags, would be almost as effective [as actually laying landmines] providing the secret was well kept'.[41] Despite these measures Richmond eventually fell to the Union.

As the industrial strength and weight of numbers of the Union forces pressed unrelentingly on all fronts, the dash of the Confederate Army was reduced to a series of grim sieges and rearguard actions. Embittered and outgunned, landmines helped them to buy that precious resource – time; but this was sufficient only to postpone the outcome of the war, not alter it. The total number of landmines used during the war was probably under 20,000 and they returned in total perhaps a few hundred casualties,

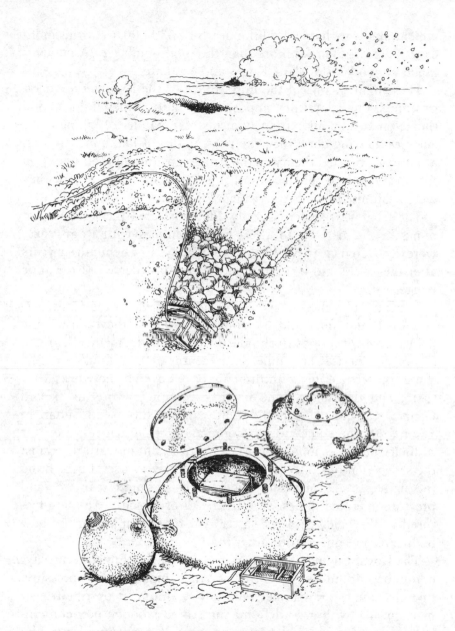

From the top – A fougasse firing, a fougasse about to fire using safety fuse initiation and a cross section showing the gunpowder charge and rock 'shrapnel'.

Bottom – landmines of the American Civil War. On the left is a 24-pound shell fitted with a Rains fuze, on the right are two electrically-initiated fragmentation mines.

which, in a war that caused the death of 620,000 seems insignificant. This last figure is more than the total number of Americans killed in two World Wars, Korea and Vietnam.

These figures conceal the importance of the lessons they demonstrated: the delays they imposed, the caution they induced and the acceptance of an extremely distasteful manner of killing one's enemies. Having confirmed the possibilities of landmines and, in a sense, legitimized their use, the Americans turned their backs on the weapon. It would be another seventy-six years before they were again used by an American soldier.

The Civil War experience also demonstrated the longevity of mines in the ground. In 1960 five landmines with Rains fuzes were recovered near Mobile, Alabama. Nearly a hundred years after they were laid it was noted that the powder was 'still quite dangerous'.[42]

In contrast to the grave circumstances in which the Confederates used landmines and the sober debate that they caused, the British Army was positively gleeful about them in their African campaigns of the late nineteenth century. 'Landmines are the thing for defence in the future. We have covered the works with them, and they have done much execution', wrote an excited General Gordon to a friend following operations in Sudan in 1884.[43] Of the same war a Commander Kingscote wrote, 'for ordinary purposes mines must be electrical, but in warfare against the savage nations, mechanical mines were very useful in fighting the natives'.[44] During these wars fougasses and tripwire- and pressure-operated mines were used. All of which were manufactured in the field, with the latter two types employing the new high explosive guncotton rather than gunpowder.

The Royal Engineers Museum at Chatham in England displays a number of mines from the Sudan campaign. The pressure-operated mines are cumbersome devices initiated by rifle-trigger mechanisms, with a crudely manufactured wooden box containing a detonator and a slab of guncotton. (Guncotton is a highly-nitrated nitrocellulose and was introduced as the standard military high explosive in the early 1870s.) Additionally, several designs of the time-honoured caltrop which were strewn around British defences at Khartoum are featured at the museum. The crude pressure devices were locally manufactured and lacked the efficient fuze mechanism employed by the Confederates some twenty years earlier. The British Army probably failed to grasp the significance of Rains's invention because the red tunic and 'whiff of grapeshot' were normally sufficient to see off the 'natives' and the thought of having to mount a serious defence was not considered.

The 'natives' were more adept at locating landmines than Commander Kingscote suggests. Major-General Sir Elliot Wood claimed that the sharp-eyed Sudanese frequently found 'observation and tripmines'. As a result 'treadmines' were manufactured; but it was also noted that their mechanisms frequently became choked with sand and the locals also developed an eye for them. A case in point featured one Lieutenant Asquith, Royal Engineers who was asked to lay 'treadmines' to cover possible sniping positions overlooking the construction of a fort near Khartoum. Checking the location of his mines on the following day, 'poor Asquith had evidently been on his hands and knees scraping to find the mine, for only his legs from knee to foot were found together untouched'. The Sudanese had evidently found and relocated mines to catch the young officer.[45]

During the Boer War, in addition to fougasses, pressure and tripwire landmines were used to defend lines of communication that were sabotaged by Boer commandos. After laying mines to protect the Blomfontein–Kruger railway, Lieutenant Musgrove, also of the Royal Engineers, noted that, 'although the line had been injured for eight successive nights before the mines were laid, it was never interfered with . . . after the first explosion'.[46] Additionally, 'mines were laid [along the roads] at nearly every culvert and had good moral effect, as after this was done, the Boers never attempted to destroy them.'[47] These tactics were hardly new to the British in South Africa. In the Zulu War of 1879 landmines and booby traps were used by engineers to protect road-building parties from attack. Engravings from the period celebrate the destruction of spear-wielding warriors by such weapons.[48]

By the beginning of the twentieth century the concept of landmine warfare had permeated through most regular armies. All types of mine were employed during the Russo-Japanese War of 1902–06, including fougasses, electrically-fired observation

21

mines and even electrically-initiated vibration- and pressure-sensitive mines. The last was a Russian invention that relied upon the depression of a wooden lid to complete an electrical circuit by disturbing a ball bearing. The electrical fuze was housed in a wooden box 2ft square with an explosive charge packed into another wooden box of similar dimensions. Several of these devices were discovered by British officers attached to the Japanese Army, but no accounts of their effectiveness exist.[49]

Conclusion

Traps, fougasses and pressure-operated landmines have a long but inglorious heritage. Their use has been moderated only by tactical demands and the technology of the period. As waterproof containers, chemical flash compositions, electrical initiation and high explosive became available, they were rapidly assimilated into victim-operated traps. While the fougasse played a minor role in the defence of permanent fortified positions, caltrops and early landmines were used by armies engaged in mobile warfare to change the ground to their advantage or in static defence to enhance fortifications. Armies adopt a defensive posture in the face of a stronger enemy and, as Caesar so clearly showed, the use of traps as part of the defence acts as a force multiplier. Caesar also demonstrated the principles of defensive barriers: concealment, depth, variety and covering with fire, which crystallized as part of current military doctrine. To the Confederates landmines became more than a simple defensive barrier. They discovered that they could provide economies in defence, impose attrition on attackers, cover withdrawals and induce caution in an advancing army, a capability previously unavailable to the military. Having proved their value, advanced the technology and overcome any moral qualms about their employment, the proliferation of the landmine was assured.

References and Notes

1. Caesar, p. 191.
2. Now more usually referred to as abatis.
3. Caesar, pp. 191–2.
4. Ffoulkes, p. 131.
5. Bishop and Coulston, p. 155.
6. Quoted in Southern and Dixon, p. 165.
7. Ibid.
8. Gillingham, p. 125.
9. Quoted in Ffoulkes, p. 131.
10. In addition to Cambodia they were also used in Korea and Vietnam.
11. Ffoulkes, p. 131.
12. Quoted in Davis.
13. McKenzie, pp. 48–59.
14. James and Thorpe, pp. 207–8.
15. Quoted in Nef, p. 43.
16. Nef, p. 44.
17. Hoppen, p. 112.
18. Trump, pp. 133–4.
19. Montross, p. 580.
20. Perry, p. 4.
21. Ibid., p. 6.
22. Quoted in Perry, pp. 33–4.
23. Ibid., p. 11.
24. *Harper's Weekly*, 29 March 1862; *Scientific American*, 5 April 1862.
25. Professional Papers of the Corps of Royal Engineers, Vol.15, 1866, pp. 26–7.
26. Ibid.
27. War Office (1902), p. 86.
28. 'Correspondence', *Royal Engineers Journal*, Vol.14, No.169, 1884, p. 283.
29. Ibid., Vol.33, No.395, 1903, p. 267.
30. Buttery, p. 264.
31. Ulrich Kreuzfeld, in *The International Military and Defence Encyclopedia*, ed. T.N. Dupuy (London: Brassey's, 1993), Vol.4, pp. 1757–8.
32. Perry, p. 21.
33. George B. McClellan quoted in Perry, p. 22.
34. Ibid., p. 23.
35. Ibid., pp. 37–8.

36. Ibid., p. 165.
37. Ibid., p. 166.
38. Quoted in ibid., p. 165.
39. Rains died at Aiken, South Carolina on 6 September 1881 aged 78, having spent his last years employed as a clerk in the US Quartermaster's Department
40. Perry, pp. 179–80.
41. Professional Papers of the Corps of Royal Engineers, Vol.15, 1866, p. 27.
42. Perry, p. 206.
43. 'Correspondence' in *Royal Engineers Journal*, Vol.14, No.169, p. 283.
44. Ibid., Vol.16, No.182, p. 52.
45. Wood, p. 161.
46. *Royal Engineers Journal*, Vol.33, No.395, 1903, p. 267.
47. *Idem.*, Vol.34, No.400, 1904, p. 53.
48. Knight, p. 94.
49. General Staff, *The Russo-Japanese War*.

Chapter 2

The First World War
and Beyond

Anti-personnel Mines

The converse of the adage 'necessity is the mother of invention' may be applied to the employment of anti-personnel mines in the First World War. Despite the massive scale of the war, the use of mines was not widespread because the new weapons of the industrial age gave rise to tactics that marginalized them. On the Western Front the opposing armies adopted defensive postures after finding themselves paralysed by the new style of warfare. The steel splintering shrapnel shell and the machine-gun had been refined to such a degree that the only option was to wage a troglodyte war from parallel rows of trenches. The muddy, cratered strip of no-man's-land, fringed with barbed wire did not require landmines to stop an infantry advance. A battalion attempting to attack was cut down in a matter of minutes by a rain of steel. The point about the machine-gun was that is *was* a machine spitting out 600 bullets per minute. Therefore any use of anti-personnel mines would have been the military equivalent of gilding the lily. Curiously, the new style of warfare was to precipitate the revival of classical military tunnelling and mining. Tunnels were dug under the enemy trenches and packed with explosives. These would be detonated immediately before an attack to breach a gap through which an incursion could be forced.

The Western Front was not entirely free from anti-personnel

mines (nor ancient forms of traps: at Ypres the Germans employed 'wolf holes' which were identical to Caesar's lily pits). Tripwire-activated mines were laced within wire entanglements early in the war but they were liable to be as dangerous to one side as the other and they were quickly phased out.[1] Throughout the war anti-personnel mines and booby traps were laid in abandoned positions in anticipation of an enemy advance. This tactic was designed to prevent the rapid reoccupation of defensive locations. In a war that has become a byword for carnage, it seems almost churlish to suggest that they were also designed to cause casualties.

Anti-personnel mines were adapted from artillery shells, although fuzes were manufactured specifically for use in this role. These were simple pressure fuzes which screwed into the nose of the shell. The shells were buried vertically in the bottoms of trenches with the fuse level with the ground.[2] Initiating such a device would mean the certain death of the activator and anyone else standing nearby.

Another type of anti-personnel device, though not strictly defined as a mine, was the long-delay action device frequently used by the Germans. This again consisted of artillery ammunition, normally the medium or heavy *Minenwerfer* shell, fitted with a chemical fuse that detonated the device up to 48 hours after it was set. These were buried in abandoned positions and roads to harass occupying forces. Their effectiveness can be ascertained from the following passage relating to the Allied advance following the battle of Sambre, 5–7 November 1918:

'A new device added to the labours of the tunnelling companies detailed to search for and remove charges, it was the delayed action fuse exactly similar in appearance to the ordinary 5.9 inch howitzer fuze except for a small mark . . . owing to these conditions, progress was much slower . . . and the opportunity to turn an unprepared retreat into a rout could not be taken advantage of.'[3]

The Allies were equally cunning in their use of mines and booby traps, as this account of the evacuation of Gallipoli indicates:

'The men in the trenches spent the last day turning every dugout into a death trap and the most innocent looking things into infernal machines. Some dugouts would blow-up when the doors were opened. A drafting table had several memorandum books lying on it each with electrical connections to an explosive charge sufficient to destroy a platoon. A gramophone, wound up and with record on, ready to be started was left in one dugout so that the end of the tune meant death to the listeners. Piles of bully beef tins, turned into diabolical engines of destruction, lay scattered about. In front of the trenches lay miles of trip mines. Hundreds of rifles lay on top of the parapet, with strings tied to the triggers, supporting a tin can into which water from another tin dripped. Flares were arranged the same way. Really I never thought the British Tommy possessed such diabolical ingenuity.'[4]

An indication of the concern about these sorts of weapon is found in the Armistice agreement of 11 November 1918. Under Article 8 the Germans were obliged to hand over plans showing where mines and delayed action charges had been placed. The information given was useful 'only as a general guide' and 'hundreds of charges were removed with a total of nearly two million pounds of explosive . . . considering the hazardous nature of the work, the casualties were slight with only one British Officer and seven Sappers being killed.'[5]

Although tactics on the Western Front confined the use of anti-personnel mines to a minor delaying role, they were used in German East and South-West Africa as both defensive barriers and as means of closing roads. The Germans used three types of device: improvised shells, a design based on a rifle trigger mechanism (similar to that used by the British in Sudan) and a type of pipe mine. The last was:

'Made by packing dynamite into a T piece of ordinary quarter-inch water pipe. A glass tube in the cross piece held the detonating compound. A thin steel rod in the long part of the T had one end resting on the glass tube; the other projected about a half inch above the ground when the mine was buried. When

27

stepped on, the rod broke the glass tube and detonated the charge.'[6]

This is significant in the history of landmines because it was probably the first operational device calculated to wound by the blast effect of high explosive rather than to kill. The South Africans fighting in German South-West Africa were outraged by their employment and on a few occasions soldiers had to be restrained from killing prisoners who had defended their positions with them.[7] Many 'trigger mines' were also laid but with less satisfactory results. They were constructed under field conditions and nervous soldiers often laid them with the safety catch left on after one of the chief armourers was seriously injured manufacturing them.[8]

Anti-tank Mines

Throughout the war attempts to endow the offensive with superior strength were largely unsuccessful. The machine-gun, so effective in defence, was difficult to use on the attack. Intense artillery bombardment did little to weaken defences. Poison gas proved too capricious a weapon and the new air reconnaissance capability robbed both sides of surprise attacks as troop concentrations could easily be spotted. Eventually tanks were developed which could maintain the momentum of an attack by combining armoured protection with firepower.[9]

The first tanks were introduced to the battlefield by the British in September 1916. They trundled forward in small groups and met with limited success, as an eyewitness to the action related:

'Instead of going on to the German lines the three tanks assigned to us straddled our front line, stopped and then opened up a murderous machine-gun fire, enfilading us left and right. There they sat, squat monstrous things, noses stuck up in the air, crushing the sides of our trench out of shape and with their machine-guns swivelling around and firing like mad ... they finally realized they were on the wrong trench and moved on, frightening the Jerries out of their wits and making them scuttle like frightened rabbits.'[10]

The experience with tanks proved indecisive until the Battle of Cambrai in November 1917 when they were used *en masse* and were able to break through the German defences. They were followed by six divisions of infantry, but after three weeks, due to insufficient support, the ground was lost after German counter-attacks. For the remainder of the war tanks were used in ever increasing numbers, gradually becoming an important factor in Allied victories. Allied plans for 1919 included the use of 25,000 tanks, a tenfold increase on the previous year; the Germans, much slower off the mark, planned for 800.

To defend against this new form of weapon the Germans first looked to natural obstacles, flooding land to create swamps through which tanks could not pass. In other places where flooding was not an option wide ditches were dug or stout wooden stockades were built to block the tanks' passage. Anti-tank direct-fire weapons were produced and the armour-piecing bullet could be effective against the early tank's modest armour. The Germans also began to develop mines for use against tanks. Early designs were, like anti-personnel mines, based on artillery shells. Shells were dug into the ground and covered with boards to form a wide pressure plate. Another design featured a pivoting board that, upon pressure from a tank track, pulled a pin from a spring-loaded striker and detonated a shell.

The early anti-tank mines were constructed by front-line soldiers and proved unreliable in use and time-consuming to lay. Soon after the Battle of Cambrai the Germans started to mass produce anti-tank mines in order to increase their efficiency. They consisted of a tarred wooden box measuring 13in by 9in in the base and 6in high, filled with about 8lb of guncotton. A spring-retained bar across the top of the mine was depressed by the weight of the tank to cause it to function.[11]

These early anti-tank mines were laid with little formality in small groups on roads or the approaches to strongpoints. Deploying mines was an infantry function with each German battalion forming its own minelaying unit consisting of one NCO and five

29

German improvised anti-tank mine.

other ranks.[12] The British tank crews seldom encountered mines, indeed, throughout the war only a handful of tanks were damaged by German mines, but the crews recognized that 'the object must always be to build long lines of barriers; single mines fail to fulfil their purpose. There is a slight possibility that the caterpillar track of the tank will strike them and cause them to detonate.'[13]

Late in the war the Germans developed a standard minefield to stop massed tank attacks. It consisted of two rows of anti-tank mines offset at 2m spacings behind a barbed wire picket fence. Attached to every third picket by a wire was an explosive charge buried 2m from the fence on the enemy side of the wire. A tank knocking over a picket would have its belly blown out by the explosive charge.[14] This layout, although undoubtedly effective, was never encountered by an Allied tank formation.

It is commonly thought that the first anti-personnel mines were laid to protect anti-tank mines. This is clearly not true as the former had been used at least fifty years before the introduction of the tank. Furthermore, the employment of anti-personnel mines under such circumstances would have been pointless. It was sufficiently rare for a tank to encounter a mine that no counter-mine capability was required and, in any case, a minefield covered with machine-gun fire would be sufficient to deter any efforts at hand clearance. Perhaps soldiers trod on and initiated anti-tank mines, giving the impression that mixed minefields had been laid.

However, early in 1919 the threat of anti-tank mines was sufficient to prompt the British to experiment with anti mine rollers attached to a 'bowsprit' in front of tanks. They were developed by the Mechanical Field Company, Royal Engineers based at Christchurch in Dorset, which was given the task of devising methods of increasing mobility support to tanks. The anti-mine rollers were little wider than the width of a tank track and their diameter was about 2ft. They rolled a path a few feet in front of the tank, detonating mines under their own weight. The low operating pressure of anti-tank mines was reflected in the small size of the rollers.

In early 1918 the Experimental Section of the Royal Engineers was asked to produce a mine for use against the German tanks that were beginning to appear on the battlefield. The design eventually used was a wooden box, 18in by 14in in the base and 8in high and containing 14lb of guncotton. It was initiated by depressing a hinged lid that operated a firing lever connected to a detonator. It appears that both the British and the German designs of anti-tank mine could be initiated with less than 100lb of pressure and therefore could be triggered by a man on foot.

The Royal Engineers also laid anti-tank minefields 'on a considerable part of the 3rd and 5th Army fronts, but it was subsequently impossible to obtain definite proof of their utility or otherwise'.[15] The efforts of the Royal Engineers were not, however, entirely in vain, on 22 March 1918 'the Germans began a methodical attack ... but as they moved down the slope to

31

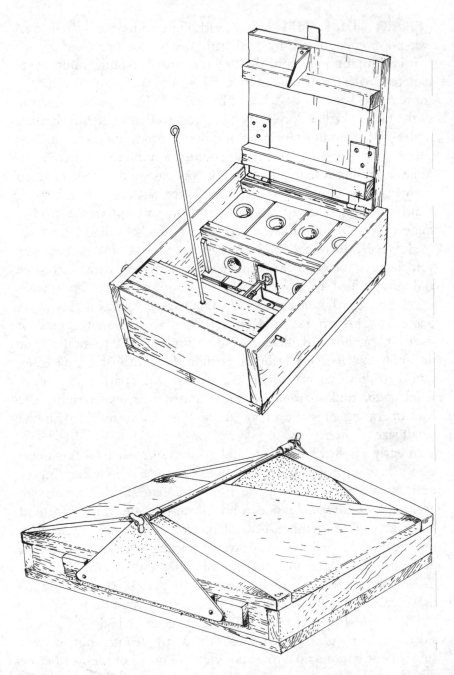

Anti-tank mines of the First World War. Top – a British mine with the pressure plate open, the vertical rod is a safety pin which was removed after the mine was laid. Bottom – a German mine.

Gouzeaucourt, their leading lines entered an anti-tank minefield and exploded some buried charges. A panic ensued and the advance was brought to a halt for a considerable time.[16] The anti-tank mine had demonstrated its worth. The same sector of minefield proved its effectiveness some months later:

> 'German minefields do not appear to have scored any great success against our tanks; in fact the heaviest recorded Allied tank casualties from mines occurred through tanks running through our own minefields laid before our retreat in March 1918 and forgotten.'[17]

The tanks involved were British Mark Vs loaned to the American 301st Heavy Battalion. Ten American tanks out of a total of thirty-five used in the attack were destroyed by mines in this incident.[18] The British mines they encountered were manufactured from trench mortar bombs augmented by 50lb of amatol, capable of destroying a thin-bellied tank.

During the First World War armoured warfare was still very much in its infancy (tanks were engaged on only eighty-three days during the entire war) and anti-tank mine warfare was at the embryonic stage of development. It was, however, clear that there was considerable potential in the use of mines as an efficient form of anti-armour weapon.

Inter-war Development

After 1918, for a variety of reasons, the development of military technology in general and of landmines in particular, was a desultory affair. The war had raised many questions about the nature of future conflict, given the new dimensions of air and armoured combat. However, the economic and emotional scars left by the war were not strong foundations upon which to rebuild military strength incorporating new technology. Even the mounted cavalry, so obviously redundant during the war, was not phased out in Britain for a full twenty years. Discussion of new technology remained until the mid-1930s largely academic and was led by the work of Captain Basil Liddell Hart who wrote a doctrine for mobile warfare based on the mobility and firepower of the tank. In terms of landmine warfare the main themes were outlined by Captain R.H. Dewing, Royal Engineers writing in 1924:

'There will be little doubt that, in the event of our being engaged in a war against an enemy armed with tanks, there will be an immediate and insistent demand for every possible form of anti-tank protection. Mines alone can never provide efficient protection, any more than barbed wire alone can be protection against infantry . . . Their value is two-fold: (i) Their physical value, arising from the power of rendering tanks immobile. (ii) Their moral value arising from the effect on the nerves on the driver of a tank of the knowledge that he may at any moment drive into a minefield . . . Three methods of destroying minefields have been suggested: (i) By artillery fire. (ii) By providing tanks with a roller . . . (iii) By a form of plough pushed ahead of a tank . . . it may be expected that some form of mechanical mine sweeper will eventually be evolved.'

All of Dewing's observations proved accurate except the last: the production of a totally effective mechanical mine-sweeping machine has eluded efforts to this day. The discussion of anti-tank warfare did prompt the Royal Engineers to design a suitable mine as early as 1928 which was vastly superior to the device put together ten years earlier. It was of a flat pear shape made of steel containing 4.5lb of TNT and was fired by depressing a knob on its top. Due to financial restraints it was never put into production. In Britain it was 1935 before small numbers of the anti-tank mine known as the Mark 1 Contact Mine[19] were produced. This contained 3lb of explosive and featured a more efficient pressure-plate design.

It is no accident that in the mid-1930s the British started to consider the potential of the anti-tank mine with some degree of purpose. Tensions were being felt throughout Europe caused by an increasingly bellicose Hitler and the threat of another major war building. In 1935 the British held their first anti-tank exercise, but suggestions that a division would require 5 to 6,000 mines across its front were met with incredulity if not ribaldry.[20] Three levels of simulated anti-tank minefield were demonstrated on the trial. The first contained 1,500 mines per 1,000yd and offered 100 per cent protection; the second, 1,000 mines per 1,000yd with 80 per cent protection; and the third, 700 mines per 1,000yd offering 50 per cent protection. The real importance of this exercise was the recognition, albeit limited, that anti-tank mines would have to be laid in large numbers and in mathematically-defined fields to stop tank attacks.

Despite these examples of advances in mine warfare the reality was that little had been achieved in practical terms by the outbreak of hostilities in 1939. As late as 1937 it was impossible in the British Army to obtain a mine for training purposes.[21] Furthermore, although anti-personnel mines of several forms had been used by the Army for decades, it was not until 1940 that they were mass-produced and they did not feature in pre-Second World War training scenarios.

Mines were used against the British in Palestine as early as 1932 and an electrical induction device carried on a pole in front of a vehicle was used to locate them. This pioneering equipment did not find its way into the main inventory of the Army and Britain entered the war without a mine detector. It seems that the British Army before the Second World War relied on expedient solutions to engineering problems with items of considerable ingenuity being assembled in the field for the duration of a particular campaign and then being forgotten.

Although this account of inter-war landmine development is confined to the British experience, with the exception of Germany (discussed in the next chapter), the development of mine-warfare capabilities in other countries was little different. Most armies remembered the lessons of previous wars but learnt little from them. By the start of Hitler's blitzkrieg in Europe, one of the few weapons capable of delaying the relentless advance of the Panzers was either left on the shelf or the drawing board.

The French had built the Maginot Line to resist a German attack but had little other hardware with which to defend themselves. In 1939 they had no anti-aircraft guns, let alone anti-tank mines. After the invasion of Poland a French anti-tank mine was produced but the stock rapidly deteriorated due to dampness and when the Germans invaded France in May 1940 these mines were never actually deployed.[22] The British also retreated before the advancing Germans without laying a mine. A British officer later remarked, 'looking back now it seems ludicrous and certainly pathetic . . . that mines were never used. There were many reasons why, but basically there were few mines and the soldiers had never seen one, let alone trained on them.'[23] The American experience was little different; it was noted that 'minewarfare was perhaps the most serious training deficit. The pre-war army failed to anticipate the importance of mines and booby traps.'[24]

References and Notes

1. School of Military Engineering (1924), p. 257.
2. Ibid. (1919), pp. 1–4.
3. Edmonds and Maxwell Hyslop, Vol.V, p. 492.
4. Norman King-Wilson, quoted in Carey, pp. 456–7.
5. Edmonds and Maxwell Hyslop, Vol.V, pp. 558–9.
6. Farwell, p. 94.
7. Ibid., pp. 92–4.
8. Gardner, pp. 157–8.
9. Foertsch, pp. 156–7.
10. Bert Chaney, quoted in Carey, pp. 464–5.
11. School of Military Engineering (1924), p. 257.
12. *Weekly Tank Notes*, Vol.1, pp. 20–6; another source suggests that as many as twenty-one tanks were destroyed by mines in this incident (Cruttwell, p. 570).
13. *Weekly Tank Notes*, Vol.1, p. 51.
14. School of Military Engineering (1919), pp. 1–4.
15. Ibid. (1924), p. 250.
16. Edmonds and Maxwell Hyslop, Vol.V, p. 492.
17. Dewing, p. 15.
18. *Weekly Tank Notes*, Vol.1, p. 41.
19. Over the next twelve years this mine had eight modifications, the last being the Mark 5 high-capacity mine which contained 8.5lb TNT.
20. Fitzpatrick, p. 26.
21. War Office (1952), p. 329.
22. Stiff, pp. 17–18.
23. Young, p. 189.
24. Doubler, p. 26.

Chapter 3

The German Influence on Landmine Warfare

After 1918 the victorious Allies turned their backs on advances in military technology, concentrating on rebuilding their shattered nations and avoiding the possibility of another war. For the Germans, the outcome of the war had been humiliating. They felt that they had not lost on the battlefield, but had been defeated in the *Materialschlacht*, the 'battle of materials'. Resentment of the harsh armistice terms created fertile ground for Hitler and his supporters to rebuild German military strength, making full use of available technology.

Having been the first nation to defend against massed armoured attacks, it is perhaps not surprising that by 1939 the Germans had also developed the most modern mines and mine-warfare techniques. They entered the war with two anti-tank and one anti-personnel mine and a firm grasp of their potential on the battlefield. By the end of the war they had manufactured sixteen different types of anti-tank mine, ten different types of anti-personnel mine and employed many different types of improvised devices and captured mines. From 1942 onwards the Germans fought almost constantly on the defensive, placing increasing importance on mines as a weapon of attrition and producing what the American General McNair claimed was 'almost a new arm of warfare'.

The German influence on mine warfare is significant because of the scale, formality and technology they used. They laid around 35 million mines during the war, a figure only exceeded by the Soviets who claim to have laid around 67 millions.[1] German mines were laid to a distinct pattern and were incorporated into the overall tactical setting in a manner immediately recognizable by students at West Point, Sandhurst or St. Cyr today. They constantly updated their mines to defeat countermeasures, introducing a new mine on average every three months during the war. German mine-warfare technology and tactics have been adopted internationally and have been surpassed only in recent years by the introduction of scatterable mine systems and electronic fuzing. Almost every aspect of mine warfare until the introduction of these modern devices originated from the Germans, with other important contributions from the Italians and the Soviets.

The German, like many other armies, was aware of the possibilities of mine warfare during the First World War but had only limited opportunity to use it. It had recognized by 1918 that anti-tank minefields should be laid in mathematically-defined patterns to ensure a high probability of a 'kill', although this was never fully tested in operations. Refinement of the tank and the introduction of blitzkrieg tactics led the German Army to think seriously about the use of mines to stop armoured counterattacks. Armour was most efficient when driven at speed to produce a 'shock action'. Minefields could not only counter enemy shock action but also stop attacks altogether if combined into the total defensive effort. In consequence, minefields were laid according to several principles: they should be marked and recorded, covered with anti-tank and small-arms fire, the depth of the fields should be such that they could not be breached in a single night, other obstacles such as ditches or wire enhanced effectiveness and a mixture of anti-tank and anti-personnel mines should be laid. 'We have learnt in our engagements with the British', wrote Rommel, 'that large minefields with isolated strongpoints dispersed within them are extremely difficult to take.'

In the First World War tanks spearheaded the attack for the infantry; but the use of mixed minefields posed something of a chicken-and-egg question for armies seeking to breach them. Who goes first, the tank or the sapper? The tank is vulnerable to anti-tank mines but protected from anti-personnel mines. The sapper is too light to initiate anti-tank mines but vulnerable to anti-personnel mines. Before tanks were adapted to clear mines it was, of course, the sapper, cheaper and therefore more expendable than the tank, who cleared the path. This eliminated the possibility of surprise attacks and created something of a symbiotic relationship between armour and engineers.

The Germans anticipated the conundrum a decade before the war with the introduction of a simple yet devious development – the anti-handling device. These were small fuzes screwed into the mine casing and anchored to the ground, thus ensuring detonation if the mine were removed. The use of, or the capability to use, anti-handling devices meant that all mines had to be treated with extreme caution, making the sapper's task especially slow and hazardous. To ensure compatibility, all screw threads on German mines were of standard sizes and lift devices and fuzes could be interchanged between different models.

Laying Minefields

In the early part of the Second World War the German Army developed a formality and method to its minelaying that was admired by the Allies. 'No one who had first-hand experience of following up a German retreat can forget the thoroughness of their methods', wrote a British officer after the war.[2] Four basic types of minefield were employed: tactical, with mine barriers in front of defensive positions; nuisance, along lines of communication; random, at bridge demolitions and positions likely to be occupied by enemy troops; and dummy fields, which gave the appearance of real minefields but contained no mines. After the war most armies adopted these types and methods themselves.

The Germans meticulously planned the location of minefields and the mines within them. All types of minefield were carefully surveyed from a reference point (*Festpunkt*), such as a road junction which could not be erased by the effects of battle. From the reference point a series of fixed points were plotted using map and compass which were then marked on the ground using steel bars set in concrete.

Mines were laid in a uniform pattern consisting of rows of anti-tank and anti-personnel mines. To measure distances between mines a measuring wire (*Minenmessdraht*) was used. This wire was 24m long, with a wooden marker tied every metre and a series of 12.5cm diameter rings tied at one end. The wire indicated the spacing at which mines should be laid, the gap between mine rows and, by using different rings, the staggering of mines from row to row. Tactical minefields were up to sixteen rows deep and were laid in 24m long panels. Mines were normally, although not exclusively, buried and camouflaged and within the field safe lanes were left open for assaulting troops.

The enemy side of a minefield was usually unmarked, but the home side was always indicated by painted signs and sometimes a single strand of barbed wire. Edges of safe lanes were marked by a vertically divided sign with a white portion on the side of the lane and a red portion on the mined (dangerous) side. Signs featured painted words: *Minen* for mines, *Gasse* for lanes and *Entmint* for areas cleared of mines.[3]

Standard forms were used to report the location and technical details of minefields. These were filled out in great detail with over twenty-five different conventional signs indicating reference points, types of mine, booby-trapped mines and the location of fences. Copies of the form were retained by the engineer unit responsible for laying the minefield, the defending unit and an additional copy was sent to a central headquarters in Germany.

Laying minefields was choreographed into a rigid drill. Fifty men, each carrying four mines, were lined up on the measuring wires and on a given signal they laid a mine at their feet. The whole line then moved forward six paces, turned left, moved three paces and laid another one. The same process was repeated with the other two mines. The whole line then went back and buried each row of mines, and then armed and camouflaged them. The same drill was used to lay anti-personnel mines once the anti-tank mines were in place. In favourable conditions an area 300m by 18m was laid in 45 minutes.[4] A typical minefield would contain a ratio of two anti-tank mines to every one anti-personnel mine and 3 per cent of anti-tank mines were fitted with anti-handling devices.

Tactical minefields were always covered with fire, normally with both small arms and anti-tank weapons. Listening posts consisting of at least two men were established on the rear edge of the minefield. Occasionally well-trained dogs were tethered to posts around a minefield to bark at the first indication of intruders. The human sentries would guard the field against enemy sappers and co-ordinate fire against infiltrators. Often they would wait until the enemy had initiated a mine or cleared to well inside the minefield before opening fire, thus providing the enemy with little opportunity to extract themselves. These tactics were clearly very effective, as an American account related:

'at the first sound of exploding mines, the Germans would lay down protective fire ... some men elected to remain erect through intensive fire rather than risk falling on a mine. Nothing was feared more than mines, they were insidious, treacherous things, hiding in deep grass and in the earth.'[5]

From 1942 onwards the Germans relied increasingly upon mines to disrupt and delay Allied forces and to inflict tank casualties. The table below indicates the soaring use of the several marks of anti-tank *Tellermine* in all theatres between 1939 and 1945:[6]

1939	1940	1941	1942	1943	1944	1945
108,100	102,100	220,900	1,063,600	3,414,000	8,535,500	–

With a total of 13.5 million *Tellermines* alone being laid by 1944 (they were replaced by *Topf* mines by 1945) it is possible to estimate the total scale of German minelaying during the war. A further 5 million anti-tank mines may have been laid during the last months of the war in 1945. *Tellermines* perhaps represented 75 per cent of all German anti-tank mines; the remaining 25 per cent were other German-designed mines or captured stocks of Allied mines. This yields a figure of around 22.5 million anti-tank mines. Assuming a ratio of two anti-tank mines for every one anti-personnel mine, perhaps around 12 million of the latter were also laid making a grand total of around 35 million mines laid in all theatres.

The Germans were correct in assuming that mines would be effective against tanks. Of 2,245 British and American tanks lost in the campaign for north-west Europe, 449 or 20.5 per cent were lost to mines, compared with 14.5 per cent that were destroyed by other tanks.[7] As an anti-tank system, the mine had clearly come of age. Mines also took their toll on foot soldiers, accounting for

41

4.4 per cent of American casualties during the war. Additionally, mines took on 'a fiendish character in the minds of [Allied] troops' and the S mine (described below) 'was probably the most feared and respected device encountered by Allied troops in World War Two.'[8]

Mine Technology

The German gift for mechanical engineering was clearly shown in their production of military equipment, and mines were no exception. Their designs followed a number of fundamental principles: safety (for the layer), reliability, economy, simplicity, counter-countermeasures and durability. They demonstrated that, in mine warfare, the designer always has the initiative and they maintained it throughout the war, thwarting each countermeasure with a new design.

As early as 1929 the first mass-produced anti-tank mine was manufactured in Germany. This was the *Tellermine* 29 (Tmi29) which contained 10lb of TNT and featured three ZDZ 29 fuzes and three anti-handling fittings. These were encountered by the Allies in all theatres during the war, but even by 1935 it had been superseded by two versions of the *Tellermine* 35 (TMi35). The most effective of these was the Tmi35 *Stahl* featuring a fluted pressure plate that covered the top of the mine. The *Tellermine* went through further modifications in 1942 and 1943, with the charge weight increased to 12lb and modifications to the fuzing mechanisms, including a blast-resistant fuze designed to negate the effect of sympathetic detonation and the new explosive clearance methods being used by the Allies. Of the five versions of the *Tellermine*, three were in production in Yugoslavia well into the 1980s and functioning *Tellermines* are still found in the North African desert to this day.

In 1940 French troops skirmishing between the Maginot and the Siegfried Line encountered a new device that leapt out of the ground and detonated in the manner of grapeshot. They considered it a secret weapon and nicknamed it the 'silent soldier'. They had discovered a new and savage form of mine: the *Schrapnellmine* 35 (Smi 35) which had been invented five years previously. The *Schrapnellmine* 35, or S mine as it was later called by Allied troops, was a significant improvement on the fragmentation devices demonstrated by Confederate troops in the 1860s. It was about the size of a beer can and was activated by a three-pronged push device or a pull igniter attached to a tripwire. When fired, a canister was launched about one metre above the ground by a blackpowder charge before it detonated, scattering 350 steel balls out to a range of 150m. A chemical-filled version of this mine was also produced but did not see service.

The first major innovation of the war was in 1942, with the introduction of wooden-cased mines. These were designed to thwart the electronic mine detector which had proved effective for the British Army in North Africa. The anti-tank version was the *Holzmine* 42 and the anti-personnel version the *Schutzenmine* 42. The latter became widely known as the *Schu*-mine and has been widely copied, especially by the former Soviet Union with the designation PMD-6. Both mines were simply constructed, reminiscent of those employed in the First World War.

The *Schu*-mine was the first, modern, anti-personnel pressure mine to be widely used (the French and the Italians had similar mines in their inventories but only limited numbers were produced). Employing the same principle as in the mines used in the German African colonies in the First World War, the explosive in a *Schu*-mine was sufficiently powerful to leave its victim limbless but not strong enough to kill him. All subsequent designs of pressure-operated, anti-personnel mines have employed this same cynical equation, the intent being to maim rather than to kill.

Although the intention seems cynical, it is also immensely practical. A smaller explosive charge is cheaper and provides other economies for manufacturers, such as a requirement for less casing material. For defending armies, smaller mines require less transport and they are easier to bury and to conceal. For attacking forces, small mines are more difficult to locate and the wounded are a greater burden on medical and transport resources than the dead. In addition it is believed that the sight of a limbless soldier in agony is more demoralizing to his comrades than a dead one, thus inhibiting aggressiveness. The Germans may have stumbled across this realization by chance. The *Schu*- mine used a standard 200g demolition charge, the smallest size available, and its use offset the requirement for additional manufacturing effort. However, nearly all subsequent designs of anti-personnel pressure mine have contained 200g or less of explosive; in battle whether a man loses his leg at the ankle or the knee is irrelevant; he is no longer a threat. The maiming rather than the killing effects of anti-personnel mines are due to practical and economic factors rather than to any particularly sadistic intent.

In addition to being difficult to locate, the use of wooden-cased mines also eased the pressure on steel supplies, an increasingly scarce resource for the encircled Germans. However, the wooden mines also used metal fuzes, nails and hinges in their construction and advances in Allied metal detectors enabled them to be located in favourable conditions. The Germans therefore started to manufacture mines from glass (*Flascheneismine*, 1942; *Glasmine* 1943), clay (1944) and bakelite (*Schutzendosenmine*, 1944). It is interesting to note that the use of glass in weapons was not entirely new: in the seventeenth and the eighteenth century hand grenades were made from it. These alternative, non-metallic containers also proved more durable in the wet soils of northern Europe than wooden mines (but in dry climates the wooden-cased PMD-6 has been found in operational condition up to ten years after it was laid), although they were never produced in great numbers. The problems of detectability and durability were solved apparently by Hitler himself, who in December 1943 ordered that a new mine should be made out of plastic. 'The other day I was thinking if it wouldn't be possible to infest the minefields with other mines, as well as anti-personnel mines, to such an extent that even our own men can't pass these minefields, because they explode no matter who steps on them. These mines should be cased in plastic instead of metal.'[9]

The new plastic mine was produced in advance of the anticipated Allied invasion of north-west Europe and was known as the Tmi 4531 or, more commonly, the *Topfmine*. In the last few months of the war it completely superseded all previous standard anti-tank mines and was the only type delivered to front-line troops. The *Topfmine* was a genuine minimum-metal mine: not only was the body made of plastic, all its other parts were made of glass, bakelite or wood, with the exception of the igniter spring which was made of metal. It contained around 8kg of amatol, was fully waterproofed and also featured the standard fitting for anti-handling devices. The Americans were to remark of their advance through northern Europe that 'particularly disturbing were the extensive nests of non-metallic, anti-personnel Schu mines and anti-tank Topf mines, neither of which responded to ordinary mine detection devices.'[10]

The *Topfmine* did, however, respond to the German *Stuttgart* 43 detector. In north-west Europe the Allies became aware that the Germans were capable of locating *Topfminen* but were uncertain how they achieved this. Early in 1945 the Allies realized that each mine was surrounded by sand and then camouflaged. They correctly assumed that the *Stuttgart* 43 was locating some special property within the sand, pouches of which were issued with each mine. It was not until after the war that a Geiger counter was run over the sand and the secret was discovered: the sand, known to the Germans as *Tarnsand*, was radioactive.[11]

A further indication of the pressures on German steel production was the introduction of the *Stockmine*. The *Stockmine* concept was similar to that of the Italian picket mine, which, unlike the Italian soldier, proved effective in the African desert. The picket mine took its name from the wooden stake that was set vertically in the ground and upon which the mine was fitted. The mine itself consisted of an explosive charge of around 75g inside a thin, metal, fragmentation cylinder. A simple fuze mechanism was attached to a trip wire and, on initiation, the charge burst the cylinder into hundreds of splinters. To conserve metal the *Stockmine* used a concrete fragmentation sleeve but was almost identical in all other aspects. The Soviets used a heavy, cast-iron fragmentation jacket for their own version of the picket mine – the POMZ[12] which remains in common use to this day. The *Stockmine* was clearly much less sophisticated than the S mine which had appeared eight years previously but was employed in the same manner.

Further efficiencies were possible by providing a mine with a higher probability of being initiated by a tank. Conventional, round, anti-tank mines with a pressure plate approximately 30cm in diameter, required a tank track to pass directly over it before it could be initiated. Increasing the size of the mine would naturally increase the chance of its being hit by a tank. The Italians were the first to put this concept into practice with their B2 and V3 barmines and the Germans used these as the basis for the *Riegelmine* 43 (RMi 43). The RMi 43 was 80cm long, 9.5cm wide (hence the term 'barmine') and contained 8kg of amatol. The pressure plate on the RMi 43 covered the entire length of the mine, making it almost three times as likely to be hit by a tank track. Therefore one-third fewer mines were required to cover a particular area, with great savings in manufacturing, logistical and laying efforts.

While barmines greatly increased the effectiveness of individual mines, the kill ratio could be enhanced further if mines could be initiated by the entire width of a tank rather than just its tracks, which represented only 20 per cent of the width. The result was the tilt rod, a vertical wooden or metal rod about 30cm long and designed to initiate a mine when struck by a tank hull. The first tilt rods were improvised from ZZ 35 pull igniters attached to the anti-handling fitting of a *Tellermine*, but having proved successful the *Kippentzünder* 43 tilt igniter was manufactured.

Having increased the initiation rate of anti-tank mines, the next step was to increase the amount of damage they caused. Anti-tank mines were designed only to break a tank's tracks, achieving a 'mobility kill' which could be repaired relatively easily. In north-west Europe only 14.5 per cent of American tanks were irreparable after encountering mines.[13] The tilt rod did not entirely solve the problem. While the detonation of a mine beneath the hull of a tank was extremely alarming and possibly injurious to the crew, it was rarely devastating to the vehicle. High explosive must be in close contact with a target if it is to cut steel, therefore the tilt rod-initiated mine had mostly concussive effects. Thus the hollow charge principle came to be applied to belly-attack mines. The hollow charge is an inverted cone of explosive lined with copper or a similar material. When initiated from the tip of the cone the liner inverts into a narrow stream of molten metal capable of piercing thick armour plating. The *Panzerstabmine* (PzStabMi 43) featured a tilt rod combined with a hollow charge and undoubtedly had great potential but its production was abandoned due to jealousies within Army departments after 25,000 had been made.[14]

Many years ahead of its time, an air-dropped, scatterable 'mine' system was produced but used infrequently throughout the war.

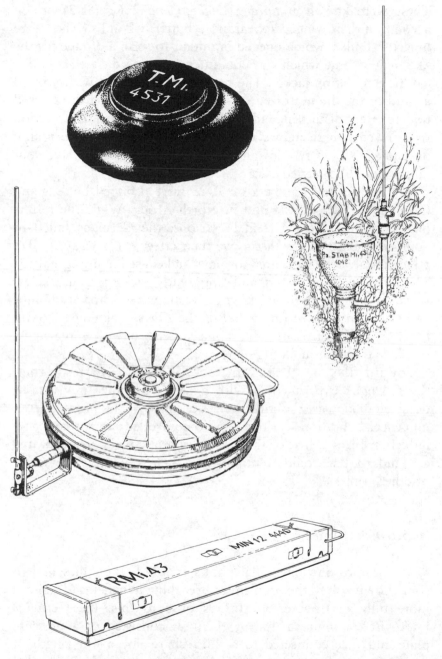

German anti-tank mines of the Second World War. Clockwise from the top: *Topfmine, Panzerstabmine, Riegelmine* and *Tellermine(Stahl) 35* fitted with an improvised tilt rod.

These were known as *Spreng Dickenwend 2 Kg* (SD2) or, on account of their winged appearance, 'butterfly bombs'. They were hinged cylinders which opened in midair to form a drogue for the 2kg main charge which was contained in a closed, steel, cylindrical, fragmentation jacket. The payload was divided with around a third of the 'mines' fuzed to detonate on impact, a third fuzed to detonate if disturbed, and the balance fitted with a delay-action fuse. Twenty-three 'mines' were carried in each container and, depending on the type of aircraft employed, up to twelve containers could be carried as cargo.

Relatively small numbers of SD2s were dropped on England (around 12,000), Russia and in North Africa. While the results on the ground were extremely serious, the Germans failed to appreciate exactly how disruptive their effect really was. An SD2 attack paralysed a wide area for days and caused many casualties. The German High Command apparently viewed them as less spectacular and therefore less effective than high-capacity bombs and their use, much to the relief of the Allies, was limited. Since the war, however, scatterable mine systems have become indispensable tools for modern armies.

Towards the end of the war, especially on the Eastern Front, the Germans experimented with a series of other innovations designed to increase the effectiveness of mines, including magnetic-influence, vibration-sensitive, radio-controlled and frequency-induction fuzes. Most of these came too late to be incorporated as standard, but would eventually find their way into the arsenals of other armies.

Improvised Mines

With the introduction of flail tanks in 1942, the Allies had to some extent solved the problem of breaching minefields (discussed more fully in Chapter 4). In response to this, the Germans improvised a mine to destroy them. It consisted of a pressure plate and fuze connected to a 44lb charge by a 4m length of detonating cord. When the pressure plate was struck by the flail tank's chains the main charge detonated under the belly of the tank. The high charge weight ensured that a precious flail tank could be destroyed. No data on their effectiveness are available but a number of these devices were found in North Africa and Europe.[15]

Other improvised mines were designed to meet local requirements. The defence of north-west Europe organized by Rommel, the architect of the North African 'Devil's Gardens', incorporated many ingenious devices. Faced with the prospect of airborne assault, poles were set in the ground 30m apart, with a proportion of them mounted with artillery shells fitted to pull fuzes, with tripwires laced between the poles. A formidable obstacle for Allied gliders but insufficient numbers of this 'Rommel's asparagus' were planted to make a decisive impact on the D-Day assault. Mines were also incorporated into the foreshore obstacles designed to deter landing ships. They were waterproofed and placed atop stakes or on cantilevers designed to press a mine against a ship's hull by lever action. Of 517,000 foreshore obstacles, 31,000 were mined.[16] In north-west France mines were also laid more conventionally, with a total of 4,193,167[17] in place along the Atlantic Wall by D-Day. The precision of this count is a further testament to the accuracy of German minefield records.

Improvised mines were also used to protect cliffs; the most curious of these was the *Rollbombe*. The *Rollbombe* was a strange item, consisting of a *Tellermine* set inside a concrete sphere and initiated by a length of safety fuse. The fuse would be lit and the *Rollbombe* heaved over a cliff, spinning towards the advancing enemy and detonating when the fuse burnt down. (Similar devices were also used by the Japanese at Port Arthur and more recently in the Bosnian wars.) Other improvised cliff mines were made from artillery shells fitted with ZZ 35 fuses anchored to stakes with slack wires. A lanyard pulled by German troops or a tripwire snagged by their enemies would cause the shell to fall and detonate when the slack wire became taut, pulling the pin from the fuze.

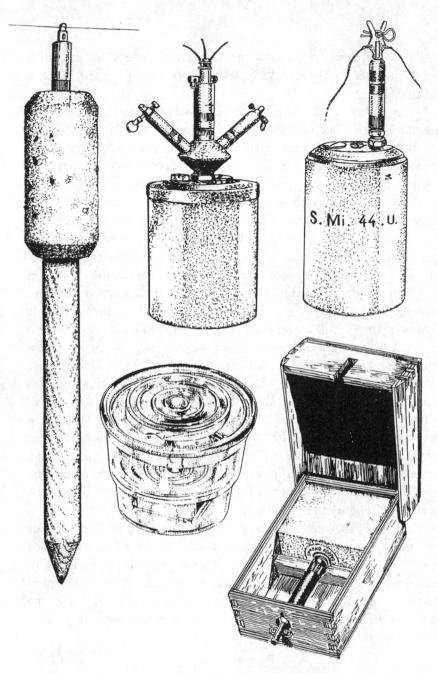

German anti-personnel mines of the Second World War. Clockwise from the left: *Stockmine, Schrapnellmine 35, Schrapnellmine 44, Schutzenmine* and *Glasmine*.

Guernsey and the Atlantic Wall

Guernsey, one of the Channel Islands occupied by the Germans during the war, was something of a microcosm of German mine warfare. An excellent account of this was given by Captain Beckingham, Royal Engineers, who led the post-war clearance of the island. Guernsey (approximately 35sq. km) was occupied in July 1940 and, although its position seemed secure, the Germans took the precaution soon after landing of planting S mines at a few strategic points. After the opening of the Eastern Front in July 1941, Hitler became concerned about the possibility of attacks on north-west France and commenced the construction of the Western Wall of which the Channel Islands formed a key part.

In total, 115 fields were laid on Guernsey, incorporating 72,866 mines, including *Tellerminen*, S mines, *Stockminen* and locally-made versions of the *Schu*-mine. Large areas of the island were planted with 'Rommel's asparagus' using captured French 300lb shells and much of the coastline featured mined underwater obstacles. Along the cliffs 518 improvised mines and over 1,000 *Rollbomben* were used. The local improvisation of *Schu*-mines along with the fact that in early 1944 6,110 mines were recovered for use in mainland France is an indication of the lack of resources available to the German Army later in the war. But it demonstrated characteristic thoroughness in marking and recording minefields. Each was marked with concrete blocks bearing an identification number that corresponded to a comprehensive plan. The plans were 'very accurate, all had serial numbers and there was a separate chart for each section of the minefield'.[18]

Conclusions

The massive increase in the number and types of mine during the Second World War, although largely German-led, was not the result of some particular characteristic of the German psyche. All armies engaged in mine warfare during the war but none mastered it like the Germans. Mine warfare was a by-product of the change

51

in military technology, principally the introduction of armoured warfare. The mine was effective in military terms and efficient economically, delaying, channelling and damaging armour while demanding fewer men and *matériel* than an armoured counteroffensive. Fighting on several fronts simultaneously, the Germans needed to enhance terrain for defensive purposes to provide economies for their over-stretched armies: a tactic used under similar circumstances by the Romans and the Confederates. A combination of necessity, technical ability and a high level of military organization ensured German primacy in mine warfare until 1945, with a legacy that survives to this day.

References and Notes

1. Zatylkin, p. 23.
2. Crothswait, p. 171.
3. War Department (1945), pp. 243–52.
4. Crothswait, pp. 171–80.
5. McDonald, p. 576.
6. H.G. Hee in Donovan and Moat, Annex B1.
7. Ibid., p. 7.
8. Sloan, p. 36.
9. Gilbert, p. 82.
10. Macdonald, p. 500.
11. Engineer Agency for Resource Inventories, Vol.18, p. 257.
12. The Russians claim to have used similar devices as early as 1916 although in only limited numbers.
13. Donovan and Moat, p.A2.
14. Burleigh, pp. 20–1.
15. War Office (1947), plate D192.
16. Liddell Hart, *Rommel Papers*, pp. 458–9.
17. Ibid., p. 310.
18. Beckingham, pp. 208–15.

Caltrops: the forerunners of landmines; concealed in long grass they were capable of inflicting painful wounds on unsuspecting infantry or cavalry. Photo: *Mike Croll*

Pressure-operated landmines (then known as 'torpedoes') were used frequently during the American Civil War; Sherman claimed that their use was 'not war but murder'. Illustration: *Harper's Weekly*, 24 May 1867

Explosion of a torpedo.

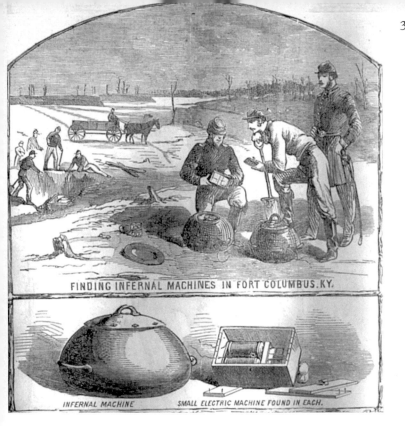

FINDING INFERNAL MACHINES IN FORT COLUMBUS. KY.

INFERNAL MACHINE · SMALL ELECTRIC MACHINE FOUND IN EACH.

3. The earliest electrically-initiated fragmentation mines were developed during the American Civil War; Harper's described them as 'infernal machines'. Illustration: *Harper's Weekly*, 29 March 1862

4. Royal Engineers preparing an improvised, electrically-initiated mine in northern France April 1918. Photo: *IWM*

5. A British tank damaged by a German anti-tank mine; only a small proportion of tanks were damaged by mines in the First World War. Photo: *IWM*

6. In response to the landmine threat experiments were conducted to enable tanks to navigate minefields safely; the first set of rollers was developed in England immediately after the war. Photo: *Royal Engineers*

7. Sappers of the Highland Division disarming German *S*-mines in the Second World War in North Africa. Photo: *Royal Engineers*

8. A British NCO supervises Egyptian workers making EP Mk VI mines in a factory near Cairo in the Second World War. Photo: *IWM*

9. Pilot vehicles were used by the British to locate minefields ahead of an advance: when a mine was detonated formal clearance began with prodders and detectors. Photo: *IWM*

10. Training in 'blind' mine clearance. Photo: *Royal Engineers*

11. The British 8th Army set up a mine warfare training school in North Africa to develop and teach breaching skills. Photo: *IWM*

12. The Matilda Scorpion flail tank, with spinning chains to beat the ground, first saw action at El Alamein. Photo: *Royal Engineers*

13. The Prime Minister Winston Churchill views a landmine display at Tripoli in
North Africa; by this point in the war the significance of landmines had
become apparent. Photo: *IWM*

14. Red Army sappers clear German
mines in the snow. Photo: *IWM*

15. A British Sherman tank with a 'bullshorn' plough; preparations for D-Day included the development of a range of rapid breaching devices. Photo: *IWM*

16. A Sherman Crab flail landing on D-Day; flails helped to breach the coastal defences and led subsequent armoured advances. Photo: *Bovington Tank Museum*

Chapter 4

The Second World War

After the Second World War, demobilized citizen soldiers introduced the term 'minefield' into everyday life, meaning a situation beset with problems. The figurative civilian expression conveyed precisely what minefields meant to soldiers of this period. The concept of mines affected soldiers deeply; they were laid without relish or moderation and encountered with fear and revulsion. During the war the mine came of age and its use shaped combat in every theatre from Okinawa to Normandy. After many false dawns mine warfare entered the field of battle on a massive scale.

The Defence of Britain

While many advances in mine warfare were the result of the German innovation, it was in fact the British who first started laying mines *en masse* during the Second World War. The British Army had fled before Hitler's Panzer Divisions at Dunkirk in June 1940 and stood isolated and vulnerable to the Nazi-dominated mainland. The scheme for the defence of Britain was explained by Major-General Martel, 'We should make every effort to prevent the enemy landing on the beach ... until he can get his heavy stuff ashore the enemy cannot do much.' Strong beach defences could reduce the number of forward troops, thus increasing the number available for the mobile reserve. Having lost a large proportion of their anti-tank weapons and with great lengths of beaches suitable for enemy landings, military planners turned to mines to assist in defence.[1]

Mines were initially laid in something of a panic. Few soldiers had even seen one and they were not used to cover the withdrawal at Dunkirk for lack of training. Consequently the beach mines were laid by untrained men with little method, inadequate recording and marking. Poor mine laying led to a number of accidents; for example, near Chichester in 1942 an infantry unit strayed into a minefield and a number of men were wounded or killed. The survivors were rescued by Major A.H. Morris, Royal Engineers who earned the George Medal for his efforts.[2]

In the event, the beach minefields were never tested, as the threat of invasion receded after the Battle of Britain was won in the air. While invasion looked unlikely after the summer of 1941, the threat was not entirely eliminated until 1943 and mine laying continued apace until then with close to 350,000 mines laid on the south and the east coast of England in around 2,000 individual fields.[3] The early mines were simple anti-tank Marks I to V but they proved unreliable in the wet conditions and the explosive charge of 4.5lb TNT was considered too small. Eventually the much more powerful Mine B Type 'C', complete with waterproof case, was adopted as the standard. The new mine contained 20lb of amatol and a bow-spring fuse mechanism set to activate under pressures in excess of 120lb.

The mining of the beaches had several unexpected consequences. As the defence of Britain became more organized it became necessary to move or to re-lay minefields. The laying of the original fields was so poor that entirely new methods of clearance, laying and accurate recording had to be devised. The difficulties of locating buried mines in the shifting sands of the beach prompted the War Office to issue specifications for a mine detector during the winter of 1941/42.

The design accepted was submitted by Lieutenant Jozef Stanislaw Kozacki, a Polish signals officer who had escaped to France and then to Britain in 1940. The Polish detector had two coils, one of which was connected to an oscillator which generated an oscillating current of an acoustic frequency. The other coil was connected to an amplifier and a telephone. When the coils came into proximity to a metallic object the balance between the coils was upset and the telephone reported a signal. The equipment weighed just under 30lb and could be operated by one man.[4] The Polish detector saw service throughout the war and the Mark 4c version was still used by the British Army until 1995.

The experience of mine warfare gained on the Home Front was to prove useful throughout the war. While the Germans dominated mine design and mine laying, the British were the great innovators in clearance techniques, initially as a result of their own short-sightedness.

East Africa

One theatre in the Second World War that is frequently overlooked is East Africa. In April 1940 Italy joined Germany against Britain and the British colony of Kenya came under threat from neighbouring Italian Somaliland and Abyssinia. The campaign was fought between Italian troops and a British force consisting of large numbers of Commonwealth troops. The Italians were almost continually on the defensive and they provided the Allies with their first taste of mine warfare. Soon after the Italian declaration of war they demonstrated the first successful use of anti-tank mines. At Sidi Azeiz an entire squadron of British armoured cars ran into an Italian minefield and the attack was halted.[5]

In September 1941 Commonwealth troops in Kenya created a defensive line to thwart an expected counterattack. Fearing Italian armoured formations 1,180 anti-tank mines were hastily manufactured in Nairobi and laid at Garissa near the Tana river. In the event the Italians did not approach – 'the bag consisted of one giraffe and an elephant' – and the mines were eventually lifted by South African sappers.[6]

Early in 1941 Commonwealth troops advanced into Italian territory from both Kenya and Sudan and started to encounter mines. While clearing mines under fire on the road to Galabat in northern Ethiopia in February 1941, Second Lieutenant Premindra Singh Bhagat of the Indian Army was awarded what was probably the first Victoria Cross for mine clearance. The Italians used V3 and B2 galvanized barmines, crudely manufactured, wooden anti-tank mines and improvised booby traps. They were laid predominantly on roads and caused some damage to Commonwealth armoured cars. During the campaign for East Africa several hundred Italian mines were lifted but they were never a major cause for concern although their potential was beginning to be realized.

Early methods for locating mines were restricted to a keen eye or a sharp bayonet, but the problem also prompted some more imaginative techniques. South African Engineers experimented with a mule-hauled contraption designed to detonate or unearth mines. It consisted of a large wooden barrel filled with concrete and coupled to a rake.[7] Although the principle was sound enough no account of its operational use survives. Perhaps even the mule had sufficient intelligence to realize that pulling a mine roller was fraught with hazard and displayed characteristic stubborness. However, the South Africans had some success at uncovering mines using a motorcycle with a steel hook attached to the back axle. When driven at moderate speeds the hook trailed on the ground and bit into any soft soil, unearthing recently buried mines.[8] The motorcycles were driven in advance of motorized columns, two abreast with the hooks trailing in the wheel ruts of the desert tracks.

The North African Campaign

The North African Campaign was a watershed for mine warfare. Before 1941 mines played only a peripheral role in combat and had a limited effect in defining the course of battle. In North Africa massed armoured formations and largely featureless terrain combined to create ideal conditions for the use of mines *en masse*. For the first time 'the battle was dominated by the tank and the mine in circumstances that favoured the former and could only be overcome by prodigal expense of the latter.'[9] Soldiers became 'mine aware', breaching drills were devised, mine-clearance machines were tested in battle and generals started to include 'mine factors' in their planning – the additional men, vehicles and time demanded to overcome the ubiquitous threat.

The campaign was limited to a coastal strip around fifty miles wide along which ran the only main road. Seaports every few hundred miles provided the sole means of supply and to the south marshes and hills restricted movement into the expanses of the Sahara. Across the coastal strip there were few features that could be used for defence and mines, along with barbed wire, offered the only means of terrain enhancement. Additionally, the problem of supplying troops across the waterless desert meant that commanders sought economies in manpower through the massive use of field defences.

The campaign was a sequence of attacks and counterattacks. In September 1940 the Italians attacked British-held Egypt but were quickly repulsed and in December the British Army advanced from Egypt into Italian-held Libya. After a series of defeats the Italians were reinforced by German forces under Rommel in February 1941. The British were eventually pushed back to El Alamein in July 1942 where they succeeded in blunting Rommel's offensive strength. In November of the same year the British regained the offensive and, after being joined by American forces in February 1943, succeeded in expelling Axis forces from Africa in May 1943. Throughout the campaign 'the side which gained armoured supremacy imposed on the other side the need for more and more minelaying as the only countermeasure available to hand'.[10]

During the first British advance mines were met in considerable numbers especially around defensive positions. Formal clearance methods had not been adopted and advancing troops kept a sharp lookout for disturbed soil and carefully probed the ground with bayonets to locate mines, as they had in East Africa in the previous year. For many soldiers their first sighting of a mine was when they uncovered one, often under enemy fire and with their own officers demanding rapid progress to maintain the momentum of an attack.

During the first phase of the campaign the Italians also used air-dropped, scatterable mines similar in principle to the German SD 2 system. On 14 September 1940 hundreds of 'thermos bombs' (named for its cylindrical shape) were dropped on British troops at Baqqush and Naghamish. The 'bomb' was fitted with an anti-disturbance fuze and detonated if it were moved. Five men were killed while attempting to move them before a protected method of clearance was improvised.[11] Like the Germans, the Italians were sceptical about the effectiveness of the scatterable system and they were seldom used again.

After the Afrika Korps arrived, the Allied advances were halted and then reversed and mines were needed to cover the withdrawal. A large number of captured German and Italian mines were employed at first but the demand continued to outstrip captured stocks or the meagre supply shipped from Britain. To overcome the problem the Royal Engineers established mine factories in Egypt to manufacture EP (Egyptian Pattern) anti-tank mines. Because of the difficulties of producing springs in Egypt a chemical fuse incorporating glass phials was used in the EP1. This along with the use of dynamite as the main charge (unstable in hot conditions) combined to create a mine which demanded extremely careful handling and production had to be stopped after 'many accidents in the hands of unskilled troops'.[12] An improved EP2 overcame many of the safety problems and hundreds of thousands were manufactured with use of local labour. Unlike the Germans, the British made no provision for booby traps in their anti-tank mines and used few anti-personnel mines. Some captured S Mines were used by the British and a copy of this German design was manufactured locally as the EP5 but only small numbers of these were produced. In Britain a bounding fragmentation mine, known in stilted military jargon as the Mine, Shrapnel Mk 1, was manufactured from mid-1940 onwards. It had a similar performance to the S Mine although it was much cruder and few were used during the war.

The British laid two types of minefield; the first was a large 'box' (some contained as many as 70,000 mines) surrounding defended positions. As the front extended, both laterally and in depth, the area between the boxes was filled with mines and became known as a 'mine marsh'. The mine marshes failed to fulfil one of the principles of defence – covering with direct fire. As the British used so few anti-personnel mines and no anti-handling devices, German tank crews were able to dismount and clear lanes in front of their tanks.

Although the British 'mine marshes' were lacking in some respects, Rommel was impressed with the total effect. 'The whole line had been planned with great skill. It was the first time that an attempt had been made to build a line of this kind so far into the desert. Some 500,000 mines lay in this [the Gazala] area alone.'[13] The British were, of course, forcing the Germans to fight in a place and manner of the former's choosing rather than fight a stronger force in an open manoeuvre battle.

Superior German strength and tactics eventually overwhelmed the Allied forces despite their prodigious use of mines. As they retreated, the Allies cleared many of their own mines for use at what would be their final effort to protect Cairo and the Suez Canal by fighting a defensive battle at El Alamein. Efforts to recover mines highlighted poor marking, recording and clearance techniques similar to those being experienced on British beaches. In December 1941 thirteen mine detectors were available to the whole Allied force – experimental Polish models – which soon proved their effectiveness.

At El Alamein in July 1942 the Allies pulled together all their resources for what was considered a last stand against the German advance. They combined an aggressive posture with static defences which incorporated hundreds of thousands of mines. Rommel's forces, overstretched and by then outnumbered, ran headlong into the defensive line and the attack petered out. The steady attrition of the Germans had succeeded in eroding their offensive strength. Although no data exist on the effectiveness of mines it must be assumed that their widespread use reflected their significant role. Indeed, when forced on to the defensive it was mines that Rommel himself sought for protection. However, when the Allies did counterattack they incorporated all the counter-mine experience learnt in the previous two years to overcome the German mines.

As a result of their experiences the British 8th Army established a mine school under Major Peter Moore, Royal Engineers. The school had three functions: to develop and teach breaching drills, to develop and teach recording methods and to experiment with new ideas. Significant progress was made on all fronts. Breaching drills centred around the use of the new mine detector with which a team of six men could clear an 8ft gap. The team comprised a detector man and his assistant, a marking tape layer, a controller and two reserves. Teams were deployed in groups of three, echeloned at 10yd intervals to clear a gap 8yd wide. They advanced at a rate of 3yd a minute which was three times as fast as prodding. The 8th Army drill forms the basis of manual clearance techniques still taught today.

Recording methods were similar to those used by the Germans, the format of which was discovered after New Zealand troops captured a German engineer officer with a minefield map. Air reconnaissance was used for gathering information about enemy minefields with some success, providing 'surprisingly good information in the otherwise featureless desert'.[14]

The school hosted 'mine awareness' courses, devised the necessary staff duties and forced the Army to consider the mine threat in a co-ordinated manner. Countering the threat for the first time became a topic for the General Staff and was considered from that time on an all-arms responsibility.

A series of new ideas were tested at the school including some of the first attempts at using vehicles for mine clearance. The earliest effort was a 'pilot vehicle' with heavily sandbagged floors designed to be driven at the head of an advancing column. This indicated the beginning of a minefield by detonating the first mine encountered while leaving the driver relatively unscathed. Lack of volunteers for this lonely and extremely hazardous occupation prompted further refinement. Spiked rollers were mounted in front of a truck and the driver operated specially extended controls from the relative safety of an armoured cab at the rear of the vehicle. Despite the additional protection, the *Tactical Employment Handbook* which accompanied them stated that 'Pilot vehicles are one-shot vehicles. Drivers of pilot vehicles are subject to considerable strain of a peculiar nature.'

The most promising tool born during the campaign was undoubtedly the flail tank. The idea for this is usually credited to the South African A.S.J. Du Toit, but it was also entertained independently by his compatriot Lieutenant-Colonel Mill Coleman.[15] Du Toit was a mechanical engineer and an enthusiastic motorist. He turned his attention to mines in August 1941 after seeing a mines presentation while on duty in the Western Desert. Du Toit was dispatched to the Armoured Fighting Vehicle Research and Development Establishment in Chobham to pursue the concept.

The flail consisted of a series of chains fixed to a spinning horizontal beam and mounted on the front of a Matilda tank. The chains were designed to beat the ground in front of the tank, disrupting or detonating mines in its path. While the theory of flailing was sound, early flail tanks had a number of shortcomings. The flail reduced the tank's performance by 30 per cent, its service life was only nine hours, it could only operate at around one mile per hour, it created enormous amounts of dust, and it was ineffective on mines buried below 4–6in. Despite these limitations it was still the most promising piece of equipment available and versions of the flail were built in England under the direction of Du Toit known as Barons and, using a similar design in Egypt under another South African, Major Girling, were known as Scorpions. Twenty-four of the latter were ready for service in September 1942.

El Alamein

Having lost the momentum of attack at El Alamein, Rommel prepared a defensive line parallel with the Allies. By this time Rommel had only 510 tanks against the Allies' 1,351 and, with the Eastern Front sucking up vast amounts of German resources, he could expect no reinforcements. His only hope was to sow his front with as many mines as possible in the hope of wearing down the Allied advance. He ordered the creation of a 'Devil's garden', a minefield so long and deep that it was considered virtually impenetrable when covered by artillery, small arms and the new and highly effective 88mm guns.

About 500,000 mines were laid in two major fields running north–south across the whole front with a total depth of about five miles. Within the minefields the bulk of the infantry and the anti-tank guns were dug in. Behind the minefields he positioned his tanks in groups so that they could move to any point of the front to prevent a breakthrough. The mines were a combination of *Tellermines*, S mines, Italian B4s and a variety of captured British models, together with an array of booby traps.

The Allied attack on the German line was named Operation LIGHTFOOT in deference to mines and began on 23 October 1942. The battle was not only named for mines, it was shaped by them. The attack commenced with the sappers employing

61

their newly-learnt drills or Scorpion flail tanks to breach lanes in the defences for tanks to charge through. The cavalry were nervous about the concept. The normal configuration for tanks to advance was in extended line thus bringing maximum fire to bear on the defenders. Attacking in file was considered suicidal, but with so many mines there was no chance of employing an extended line.

As expected, the breaching of the German defences proved difficult and costly, Brigadier Roberts commanding 22nd Armoured Brigade recalled:

> 'We tried for the first time to use what were called "Scorpions" . . . and they were very unreliable . . . they broke down and got in the way and then the Sappers had to [clear the minefields] by hand – there was a great deal of delay. And after the first night we'd all got through what was the first minefield. And then we sat between the two minefields and [the Germans were] there . . . absolutely looking down on us. It was a most uncomfortable situation.
>
> 'And then we tried again the next night . . . and we went where the gap was and . . . every tank was knocked out either by mines or anti-tank fire. We struggled all night and made no progress. And so we called it off.'[16]

While flails had mixed fortunes in breaching paths through the minefields, they did have an unexpected result. Prisoners reported after the battle that they were less frightened of the artillery barrage than the 'slowly advancing pillar of dust, out of which came dreadful noises of clanking, groaning and rattling chains'.[17]

The difficulties in breaching German minefields threatened to halt the attack. As the pressure to maintain momentum increased a regiment of forty-three tanks of the 10th Armoured Division was ordered to attempt to fight its way through the minefields, losing twenty-eight in a failed attack.[18]

Other breaches were more successful. Breaching convoys with a pilot vehicle in front followed at distance by vehicles containing sappers drove forward until the pilot vehicle hit a mine. The sappers then carried out the drills they had learnt – under enemy fire. One officer recalled, 'The great thing about our drill was that I never had to issue an order as every member knew what to do.'[19] On the first two nights of the battle some breaches did succeed in crossing the minefields although the casualties were heavy and many of the leading tanks were knocked out by enemy fire. In many places Engineers cleared lanes by prodding, which ultimately proved to be the most successful technique. While breaches were achieved, the canalization imposed upon the attacking forces prevented them from applying the maximum pressure on the defenders.

After two days of attacks the Allies were almost completely bogged down by the minefields. The situation was saved by an error on Rommel's part. He launched a counterattack against the same defences that had stopped him two months previously and weakened his forces so severely that the Allies were able to break through the 'Devil's gardens', thus forcing Rommel to stage a fighting retreat.

German Withdrawal

The Germans fought their way back to Tripoli where, on 12 May 1943, their resistance came to an end. The withdrawal was covered throughout by the extensive use of mines which took their toll on Allied forces and provided the newly-arrived Americans with their experience of modern mine warfare. One American officer stated that he 'had never seen a German mine, picture or model before entering combat'[20] – a common situation in all Second World War armies.

German mining during the withdrawal was much more dispersed than at El Alamein and often took the form of nuisance mining and booby trapping. In particular, roads, likely resting areas and demolition sites were mined. Metal scraps were scattered around mined areas to slow down detection teams and attractive items such as binoculars were booby trapped. One of the most effective techniques was to bury mines too deep to be detected. Dozens of trucks would pass over them until the ruts became deep enough for a vehicle to apply sufficient pressure finally to detonate the mine.

When the Germans did mount a formal defence they continued

to use mines with devastating effect. At Medenine in Tunisia on 9 March '201 Guards Brigade made their disastrous attack . . . we watched them arrive in fine order – their vehicles clean, the men properly dressed and the convoy discipline perfect. Hundreds of Guardsmen were killed or wounded in the attack, mainly by anti-personnel mines, and the success signal fired by those who reached the objective only served to bring the supporting carriers on to the anti-tank mines.'[21]

All available airstrips were mined and ploughed to prevent the Allies from making use of them. 'They even went as far, with true Teutonic frightfulness, as to dig shallow latrines on the runways in which before use they placed mines. They finally filled them in and made good the surface. It has to be remembered that the Sapper, after the mine has been detected, has to grub with his hands round and underneath the mine to disconnect any anti-lifting device. Such an experience does not add pleasure to an already nerve-racking job.'[22] The new types of German wooden anti-tank mine (described in Chapter 3) were used during the retreat and, as the effectiveness of the flail started to increase, linked charges designed to defeat these ensured that the Germans maintained the initiative against the countermeasures.

The continual threat of mines severely tested the Allies, although it never threatened to change the course of battle as it had so nearly done at El Alamein. The strain fell in particular on the Engineers about half of whom were constantly engaged on mine clearance operations, although during the advance the doctrine of 'all-arms responsibility' alleviated some of the burden. A War Office report[23] stated that there was 'an enormous physical and nervous strain upon the Sappers who have been referred to as "housemaids armed with Hoovers". The deliberate, continuous sweeping with detectors, each man going forward slowly and intently, eyes on the ground, earphones on the head, while the noise of battle crashes around, and the cold-blooded investigation and lifting of mines, never knowing when some heathenish invention for catching one out would not blow the grubber to eternity is a terrific strain.' After the war the Royal Engineers commissioned the artist Terrence Cuneo to immortalize the image of the cool-headed sapper operating a mine detector, concentrating intently, while a violent firefight rages around him; the painting hangs in the Officers' Mess at the Royal Engineers headquarters, Chatham.

Modest efforts were made to clear the redundant minefields after the Germans had been expelled and a visionary recommendation was made in a British report on the 'Engineer Lessons from the North African Campaign'. It was suggested that the British should design a new form of mine capable of 'self-destroying after a certain period to avoid the need for lifting'. It would take over four decades before any serious efforts were made in this direction.

During the campaign for North Africa 19.5 per cent of Allied tank casualties were attributed to mines[24] plus an estimated 5–10 per cent of personnel casualties. General officers were not immune from the threat. At least seven officers of that rank became casualties on both sides, including General von Bismarck, Commander of the 21st Panzer Division, Major-General Lumsden, Commander of 1st Armoured division and Brigadier F.H. Kirsh, Chief Engineer of 8th Army.

The casualties do not reveal the full extent of the role of the mine in this campaign. They dictated the pace and the style of the battle in the first real encounter between armour and mines. They inhibited manoeuvre, induced caution and imposed a huge logistical strain upon both sides. Yet the methods of countering mines formed the basis of those used in later campaigns and promising advances were made.

The Eastern Front

One of the bitterest campaigns of the Second World War was fought on the Eastern Front. The campaign opened in June 1941 with the German invasion of the USSR. The offensive was halted, with enormous casualties on both sides, at the gates of Stalingrad and Moscow. The Soviet winter offensive in 1943 reversed the tide of battle, eventually pushing the Germans back to Berlin. The wide expense of the east European plain 'appears to offer the invader, particularly the mechanized invader, free movement at will',[25] which could only be inhibited by the use of mines, a weapon both the Soviets and the Germans used by the million.

The Soviets, as we have seen, had experimented with mines for many years, but by 1941 they had only around a million of their TM38 anti-tank mines available for defence. They saw little requirement to spend time or money on improving equipment that had already been tested and proved reliable and consequently they copied or refined many of the German mines that they encountered. By the end of the war they had employed more than fifteen types of anti-tank mine and twelve types of anti-personnel mine. Engineer battalions with the sole purpose of laying mines (or 'cucumbers' as they were referred to in the soldier's vernacular) were formed, often enlisting civilians, including women, to assist with the work.[26]

During the course of the war the Soviets claimed to have laid 25 million anti-tank, 40.5 million anti-personnel and 1.5 million 'special purpose' mines.[27] Other sources claim that as many as 222 million were laid, but this is unquestionably an overestimate. Even the more modest figure of 67 million is probably an exaggeration. At the widest point western Russia measures 1,500km; 67 million mines are sufficient to cover this width at a density of over 44,000 mines/sq. km. Even allowing for fluctuating front lines the figure seems improbable. Whatever the real numbers, mines definitely played a significant role in the defence of the Soviet Union and imposed a huge strain on the Germans. As the German General Gunther Blumentritt drily remarked, 'the Russian predilection for large minefields is well known.'[28]

At Kursk, one of the great turning points on the Eastern Front, around half a million mines were used to halt the German attack. These were laid at an average density of 1,500 anti-tank and 1,700 anti-personnel mines per mile of front.[29] In addition to the preplanned defences, the Soviets were flexible enough to lay mines during attacks to enhance existing fields. The mines accounted for 'over a thousand tanks and hundreds of men killed' during the epic battle.[30]

The Soviets were also perhaps the first to use mines as an offensive weapon. Groups of partisans operating behind the German front frequently laid minefields in troop harbour areas or along roads to disrupt resupply and damage morale. In addition to standard mines, more advanced delay and radio-control mechanisms were used. To counter these guerrilla tactics the Germans established a mine-reporting agency offering two choices to Soviet citizens in occupied areas: a cash incentive was given to those who reported mines, but if a mine were not reported inhabitants suffered capital punishment. For example, on 29 November 1941 fifty males from Simferopol were shot for not reporting a mine which killed a German soldier.[31] To ensure safe movement the Germans also drove cattle, prisoners of war or local inhabitants in front of German soldiers in suspect areas.

Apparently the Soviets also employed dogs to deliver anti-tank mines to their targets. The unfortunate creatures were trained to associate the underbelly of a tank with food. When German tanks approached, dogs would be sent off in their direction with a tilt-rod-operated charge on their backs. While investigating the tank in search of a meal the tilt rod would initiate the charge, destroying the tank along with the dog and its imaginary dinner.

The Germans used large numbers of mines, initially to protect their own advances and flanks and then in vast quantities on the defence to grind down the Soviet advance. Rommel, in a conversation with Bayerlein, outlined his proposals for mining the Eastern Front thus:

'Now, let us suppose that the Russians attack in a heavily-mined sector where our anti-tank guns are forming a screen, say six miles deep, then – for all their mass of material – they are bound to bog down in the first few days and from then on they will have to gnaw their way through slowly. If the enemy makes more than three miles progress a day, we'll build six miles depth of anti-tank screen.'[32]

On the advance the Soviets did not prove as ingenious as their Allies in the Western Desert at devising countermeasures. However, they did produce several detectors including the VIM 625 which slotted into the muzzle of a rifle, experimented with tank-mounted rollers and manufactured wooden treadways to place across minefields. In preparation for an attack both the Soviets and the Germans relied on artillery to disrupt minefields. The Soviets used a standard firing pattern using four 76mm guns firing a total of 500 rounds to breach a gap 8m wide and 100m metres long in around 65 minutes.[33]

Many accounts of the Soviet offensive refer to the ability to sustain massive casualties, irrespective of minefields. Several reports suggested that the Soviets drove prisoners of war through minefields ahead of an attack or simply ran through them themselves, apparently willing to take casualties. Soviet engineers' attempts to clear minefields could never be achieved quickly enough for infantry and armour and in their haste, a Soviet prisoner explained, 'engineers taking part in an attack are almost inevitably wiped out'.[34] The Germans also noted the difficulties the Soviets had in minefields:

'At the Bobritsa bridgehead the good effect of our mines could be noted over a long period. Russian tanks moved into the minefield, were damaged and stopped. Heavy casualties were also inflicted on strong enemy assaults which entered the minefield. Even when the terrain was favourable, the Russians did not resume their attacks either with tanks or infantry, so that our infantry enjoyed a substantial respite. This success is ascribed exclusively to mines.'[35]

Comparing tactics on the Eastern Front with those in North Africa Rommel said:

'The Russian is stubborn and inflexible. He will never be able to develop the well-thought-out, guileful method with which the Englishman fights his battles. The Russian attacks head on, with enormous expenditure of material, and tries to smash his way through by sheer weight of numbers.'[36]

Indeed, sheer weight of numbers eventually prevailed. Both the Soviet and the German casualties on the Eastern Front were staggering, although what percentages of these were directly attributable to mines is open to speculation. It is safe to assume that, given the manner in which Soviet armour was thrown at minefields, their casualty rate was far higher than the 19.5 per cent of Allied tanks claimed by mines in North Africa.

The campaign for the Eastern Front demonstrated the value of mines to the Soviets, a lesson which had far-reaching consequences. Realizing their significance, they embarked on a defence policy which promoted the use of mines on a similarly massive but more organized scale and promoted it throughout the Warsaw Pact. By the early 1970s it was claimed that 'no other modern nation has surpassed the Soviet Union in the effective employment of landmine warfare'.[37] This expertise was passed on to satellite states in the developing world with, as we shall see, devastating results.

Sicily and Italy

Allied troops landed on Sicily in July 1943 and, after a forty-three-day campaign, invaded the Italian mainland. Soon afterwards the Italians surrendered and the Germans maintained a dogged defence, gradually retreating until they finally surrendered in April 1945. In Sicily mines were a persistent nuisance but rarely a menace; however on the mainland the pattern of mining changed. The mountainous terrain of the country restricted tanks to valleys and these areas were heavily mined. Additionally, the Germans started to abandon their careful, meticulously-planned and recorded fields and employed a much more haphazard, almost indiscriminate style, a clear indication that they had no hope of advancing again.

> 'The scale of anti-personnel mining increased as the campaign progressed. Booby traps were planted in bunches of grapes, in fruit and olive trees, in haystacks, at road blocks, among felled trees, along hedges and walls in ravines and valleys, hillsides and terraces, along beds and banks of streams, in tyre or cart tracks along any likely avenue of approach, in possible bivouac areas, in buildings that troops might be expected to enter, and in shell or bomb craters where soldiers might be expected to take refuge. The Germans placed mines in ballast under railroad tracks, in tunnels, at fords, on bridges, on road shoulders, in pits, in repaired pot holes and in debris. Field glasses, Luger pistols, wallets and pencils were booby trapped as were chocolate bars, soap, windows, doors, furniture, toilets, demolished German equipment, even bodies of Allied and German civilians and soldiers.'[38]

The Americans arrived in Italy in full force and to many of them the employment of mines came as a shock. The campaign 'revealed that minewarfare was one of the US Army's worst Achilles' heels and that troops lacked proper training and equipment to detect and clear minefields'.[39] Some had attended a British Army mine-training school in Morocco which, in its efforts to recreate realism, succeeded in causing twenty-eight casualties, including one fatality.

Mines in Italy created new challenges for the Allies. The Germans started to use increasing numbers of *Schu* mines and Italian bakelite *Pignone* mines which were virtually undetectable by electronic detector. To compound their difficulties, the Allies found that their detectors, including the new American SCR-625, were unreliable in wet weather, a problem not encountered in the African desert. Furthermore, the presence of iron ore in much of the soil caused detectors to sound alarms constantly and the Allies were once again reduced to carefully probing for mines. Probing, however, is an inexact science and a number of mines were missed by clearance teams. The New Zealanders suffered a major blow when their Divisional Commander, Admiral Kippenburger, stepped on a *Schu* mine while walking through a 'cleared' lane at Monte Trocchio.

Unlike the featureless desert, the Germans could blend minefields into natural obstacles such as rivers and steep mountain slopes, severely limiting offensive operations. Bulldozers were frequently used as an expedient clearance method, the blade pushing aside the top few inches of soil to leave a clear path for following troops. Operators wore 'flak suits' to protect against S mines, but even so it was a terrifying occupation. 'More than fifty [American] bulldozers struck mines during the campaign. In many cases operators were thrown from their seats, but none were killed. Some had broken legs, but had they been in cabs with roofs many would have had their necks broken or skulls fractured.'[40] In some instances sheep or goats were herded into minefields to clear tripwires, thus minimizing the risk to operators. In 1944 both the American and the British Army made the logical progression of fitting dozer blades to tanks.

Even clearing mines away from the fighting proved difficult enough as the American 10th Engineer Combat Battalion discovered when working on a minefield at Formia-Gaeta, north of Naples. It suffered fifteen fatalities and forty-three wounded during a sixteen-day operation to clear 20,000 mines of all types. While transporting captured enemy mines the 109th Engineer Battalion lost twelve men killed in a single explosion. It was small wonder that troops developed a loathing for mines.

In an effort to overcome the difficulties of clearing mines in Italy some useful techniques were developed. The most promising and enduring was a rifle grenade that propelled a length of detonating cord across a minefield. This innovation by the American 48th Engineer Combat Battalion left a well-defined path about 18in wide, cutting trip wires and initiating most of the *Schu* mines in its path. The bangalore torpedo, developed in that city by engineers in 1912, also proved useful in certain circumstances as did large versions, known as Snakes. Developed by Lieutenant-Colonel Willot, Canadian Royal Engineers, the Snake was made from sections of explosive-filled pipe 15ft long and 4in in diameter. It was originally designed to be rocket-propelled from a tank for a few yards then to detonate, allowing the tank to advance through the cleared area before firing another Snake. The rocket mechanism proved unreliable and the system was adapted so that lengths of Snake could be joined together and then shunted into a minefield by a tank.

The British continued to use flails in Italy, slowly improving the concept and making them more effective. The Americans attempted to make their own version of the flail known as the T3. Unfortunately, they were not as durable in combat as they appeared in tests in America. Thirty T3s were sent to Italy in spring 1943 but were soon discarded because of difficulties with the boom hydraulic systems.[41]

When forced to defend, as they were at Anzio, the Allies were themselves forced to use mines. However, they lacked the discipline and experience of the Germans and 'they planted mines haphazardly and made incomplete and inaccurate records ... the result was a marked increase in casualties'.[42] A method of laying mines was hastily improvised by the Americans, using teams of four men to lay each row. One man marked the position for each mine to be laid, one man placed the mines and two men armed and camouflaged them. It was, they discovered a time-consuming

71

process; in April 1944 a platoon of the 109th Engineer Combat Battalion took 240 man-hours to lay 2,444 anti-tank mines and 199 anti-personnel mines and an additional 96 man-hours to mark the minefield. Rather than risk placing anti-personnel mines around anti-tank mines, the Americans placed anti-personnel mines in front of a barbed wire fence and laid anti-tank mines behind it.

The Americans also discovered the error of laying mines too close together. A single mortar bomb detonated an entire mine-field laid by the 39th Engineer Combat Regiment near Anzio. Thereafter mines were laid at a maximum density of 1.5 anti-tank mines per yard of front and 1 anti-personnel mine per three yards of front in staggered rows in an approximation of the German pattern.[43] The Americans used M1A1 and M7 anti-tank mines and M2 bounding fragmentation anti-personnel mines. The British used the Hawkins light anti-tank mine and the Shrapnel mine Mark 2. Both American and British mines were crude in comparison with the well-engineered German equivalents.

In the North African desert the Germans proved that mines could create artificial obstacles; in Italy they demonstrated that mines could be even more deadly if used to enhance natural obstacles. Thirty per cent of Allied tanks and 4.4 per cent of personnel were lost to mines during the campaign for Italy,[44] underscoring their significance as a major anti-armour weapon and a significant threat to foot soldiers. The Allies were severely challenged by mines and discovered that they were poorly trained and equipped to deal with them. Much thought was given to countering the threat but the difficulties remained: a testament to the problems posed by mines rather than the efforts made to counter them.

The War against Japan

This war in its essence was fought on two fronts: in Burma and on the islands of the Pacific. In Burma the dispersed style of fighting and lack of prior experience of mine warfare by both sides meant that mines were seldom used. On the Pacific islands the geography and the method of combat lent themselves to mine warfare. Beaches were an ideal place for mines: flat, easily covered by fire and obvious routes for amphibious forces. Many islands were covered with dense vegetation with narrow tracks offering the only means of penetrating inland, another obvious area for mines. This meant that a high proportion of the terrain suitable for vehicles was mined and resulted in heavy losses.

Japanese mine warfare lacked the sophistication and formality of that of the Germans. Many of their mines were improvised from artillery shells or other munitions. They did, however, produce the effective Type 93 anti-tank mine, suitable for inland operations and an innovative beach mine. The beach mine was a hemisphere 20in in diameter containing 46lb of explosive. The mine was detonated by pressure applied to one of two horns which protruded from its sides. It was laid in several feet of water or on the beach itself and was extremely potent against landing craft or vehicles, as the following account of the assault on Corregidor during February 1945 recalls:

'Black Beach was mined. Rows of 130 anti-vehicle mines were spaced seven to fifteen feet apart along one hundred and twenty-five yards of beach. All were of a kind that poked their firing mechanism out of the sand and the infantrymen skipped over them, keeping a sharp eye out for trip wires as they ran inland. But against vehicles they proved extremely effective. One of the first out, an M7 self-propelled gun hit a mine, so did an M4 Sherman tank and a jeep towing a 37-mm anti-tank gun. Mines cost Colonel Postlethwait (Commander of the 3rd Btn, 34th Infantry Regiment) twenty-nine men and about half his vehicles.'[45]

The problem of mines was partly alleviated by the use of bulldozers with 'V' shaped blades that could doze a path across a beach and through the jungle, bypassing any mines on the existing tracks. Despite this tactic, the Americans lost 31 to 39 per cent[46] of their tanks and around 1 per cent of personnel[47] to mines during the battles for the Pacific islands. The relatively low number of personnel casualties reflects the limited emphasis placed by the Japanese on anti-personnel mines and the difficulties of siting protective minefields around dispersed positions in areas of dense vegetation.

Preparing for D-Day

In response to fears of an Allied invasion of north-west Europe, Hitler ordered the building of the Atlantic Wall. Late in 1943 he placed Rommel in charge, stressing that 'When the enemy invades in the west it will be the moment of decision in this war, and the moment must turn to our advantage.' Rommel understood the magnitude and the difficulty of the assignment; after an initial assessment in December 1943 he told his chief engineer officer General Wilhelm Meise that, due to Allied control of the air:

'Our only possible chance will be at the beaches – that's where the enemy is always weakest. I want anti-personnel mines, anti-tank mines, anti-paratroop mines. I want mines to sink ships and mines to sink landing craft. I want some minefields designed so that our infantry can cross them, but no enemy tanks. I want mines that detonate when a wire is tripped; mines that explode when a wire is cut; mines that can be remotely controlled and mines that blow up when a beam of light is interrupted.'[48]

To defend the entire coast of France and Holland the Germans were extremely thinly spread and mobile reserves operating over such a broad area were unlikely to be able to counterattack with sufficient speed. Rommel therefore favoured putting all efforts into stopping the invasion on the beach and creating a narrow defensive strip inland to fight off airborne troops. Rommel became almost obsessive about mines:

'for the first stage, that is a thousand-yard strip along the coast and a similar strip along the land front, ten mines a yard will be required, making a total for the whole of France of 20 million mines. For the remainder of the zone [8,000 yards], France will require in all some 200 million mines.'[49]

In the event, by the end of May 1944 only 4,193,167 mines had been laid, insufficient to satisfy Rommel, but enough to concern the Allies (see Chapter 3).

Throughout the war mines had caused the Allies a great deal of anxiety and it was always easier to see the problems caused by mines than to overcome them. Preparations for D-Day included a considerable amount of effort to overcome German minefields. The most promising solutions to the breaching of minefields under fire were flails, rollers and ploughs. The development of these efforts was placed under the command of Major-General Percy Hobart and these and other specialized vehicles became known as 'Hobart's funnies'.

Since El Alamein substantial effort had gone into improving the concept of flail tanks. In 1943 a flail was built around a Valentine tank and named the Valentine Scorpion. One hundred and fifty of these were built and used for training purposes. The superior Sherman Mark V was selected as the basis for the flail tank for the D-Day landings. Known as the Sherman Crab, it had a clearance speed of 2.2kph, could clear a lane 3m wide and had a significant advantage over the original Scorpion in that it retained its main armament. Six hundred and eighty Sherman Crabs were available for D-Day and subsequent campaigns.

The method of employing flails was substantially revised for operations in Europe. Flail troops consisting of five tanks were organized, three flails operated together in echelon clearing a lane 24ft wide and the other two provided covering fire or reinforcement as required. During the Normandy campaign the flail design was modified to enable the boom to maintain a steady height above the ground. This 'contouring' method helped to counter the problem of mines in depressions being missed by the flail.

The Canadians produced a useful tool in the Canadian Indestructible Roller Device (CIRD); this was attached to the front of a tank and was designed to detonate mines in its path. While they were reasonably effective in this they were not as indestructible as their name suggested and the connecting gear to the tank was frequently badly damaged. The CIRD was often used in a reconnaissance role, rolling ahead of an assault until it detonated a mine, at which point it would withdraw and flail tanks would advance and clear a lane.

The Americans also produced a roller equipped with disks 8ft in diameter, known as the T1E3 or Aunt Jemima. Instead of being pushed, the disks were mounted on the front sprockets of a Sherman tank. Disks of this size were less prone to damage but more difficult to repair. Being mounted on the front sprocket made them more manoeuvrable but, weighing 30 tons, they had difficulty negotiating muddy roads and damaged bridges. The T1E3 was not used on D-Day but a few did see limited service in Europe; one irate divisional commander described it as 'the most effective road block in Europe'.[50]

Bulldozers had been used as an expedient clearance method in North Africa and Italy. In Italy the logical progression of attaching a blade to a tank was realized and the concept was further improved for D-Day. The British produced several plough designs, including the Farmer Deck, the Jefferies and the Bullhorn. All of these were capable of unearthing mines across the track width of a tank and depositing them in windrows on either side.

Explosive methods of clearance, including the Bangalore torpedo and the Snake, were perfected for the invasion. A British innovation known as the Conger was operational by D-Day. This was a rocket-propelled hose which was fired across a minefield and then pumped full of nitroglycerine and detonated.

The explosive clearance of minefields using aerial bombardment was thoroughly tested in 1944 by the Americans on military reserves in Florida and Virginia. Nine B-17 and nine B-29 aircraft each dropped ten 350lb Mark 47 bombs (180 bombs in total) from between 8,500 and 7,600ft. The result was a breach 55ft wide across the 300ft deep minefield. The rates of clearance were: 100 per cent of *Tellermines*, 95 per cent of *Schu* mines and 76 per cent of S mines. The conclusion of the experiment was that, while it was possible to breach a minefield, the execution was technically difficult and the results were unsatisfactory as they left mines uncleared and the cratered ground was difficult to cross.[51]

Other clearance methods tested included the mounting of banks of machine-guns on top of tanks and firing them into the ground; a series of hydraulic shock-absorbed plunger rods that could be raised and lowered rapidly to pound the ground in front of a tank; and the use of heavy steel slabs hanging from a boom on the front of tanks. A vehicle-mounted detector, the AN/VRS-1, was issued to some units but never inspired much confidence. The detector was 6ft wide and an automatic control mechanism stopped the vehicle whenever the detector gave an alarm. Like its hand-held cousin, it could not detect minimum-metal mines and it constantly yielded false alarms on bomb fragments or other metal debris.

For the actual invasion the Americans preferred to use detectors, bayonets and Bangalore torpedoes, supported by armoured bulldozers, to breach minefields. The British supplemented their basic breaching tools with flails and rollers which were complimented by others of Hobart's 'funnies', including bridging tanks and fascine carriers. The American refusal to use British funnies led to a long-lasting debate; Liddell Hart claimed that 'the American troops paid dearly for the higher commander's hesitation to accept Montgomery's earlier offer to give them a share of Hobart's specialized armour ... in the event they missed the Crabs the most.' Among the Americans there was a feeling that the British were relaying too much on gadgets and not enough on brawn.

D-Day

The first assault on France was from the air by glider and parachute. There was considerable concern before it about the effects of Rommel's 'asparagus' – the lattice of poles laced with wires connected to explosive charges. Some commanders feared that these obstacles would account for as many as 70 per cent of landing casualties. In the event, the effects of the asparagus were overshadowed by the immense Norman hedgerows which split open many gliders and landing casualties were only around 16 per cent.[52]

The amphibious force had to cross an obstacle-infested surf before putting men on the beach. The obstacles included heavy iron frames known as 'Belgian gates', hedgehogs made of three lengths of railway line welded at their centres, and a row of heavy logs driven into the sand at an angle pointed seaward with a *Tellermine* lashed to the top. Underwater demolition teams had been trained and deployed to clear lanes through these obstacles but achieved little as the German snipers concentrated their fire on them. The British landing at Gold Beach had twenty landing craft struck by these mines, causing moderate to severe damage and losing men and equipment.

On the beaches and in the dunes there were more mines. Men from the 237th Engineer Combat Battalion were trying to get off Utah Beach under pressure from tanks and men behind them also trying to get off the beach. Sergeant Vincent Powell recalled, 'Those were the first men inland and suddenly they started stepping on mines, S mines, Bouncing Betties. These mines bounced up and exploded. The men began screaming and running back to the beach with the blood just flowing.'[53] On Omaha Beach the 115th Infantry Regiment were stalled for several hours when a rumour swept through the troops that American detectors could not locate German mines.[54]

Overall casualty figures for D-Day do not show what percentage was due to mines; but some indication is provided by the examples of the American 8th and 22nd Regiments on Utah Beach who had 'astonishingly light casualties' with 12 men killed and 106 wounded, 'Nearly all were caused by mines . . . mostly those devilish S mines.'[55]

The British drove their flails off the landing craft and began flailing immediately, up through the dunes and then back to the high-water mark. 'We were saved by our flail tanks, no question about it', claimed Major Kenneth Ferguson. Direct, quantifiable comparisons between the clearance methods employed are impossible to make, but it appears probable that flails did provide significant benefits to the British.

However, by nightfall on D-Day, 175,000 Allied troops were established on the beachhead at a cost of around 4,900 casualties. The Atlantic Wall, with its reinforced concrete defences, thousands of obstacles and four million mines, had held up the invaders by no more than a few hours. Could it therefore be surmised that Rommel's mines were simply a waste of time and effort? Given the length of coastline to be defended and the limited resources available, mines offered Rommel his only hope. It must be remembered that the *Kriegsmarine* and the *Luftwaffe* did not take part in the defence and many of the troops were third-rate youngsters and oldsters or not even German, although some were hardened veterans. An American soldier, John Slaughter, recalled a German prisoner being interrogated inland at Vierville:

> 'The captive was on his knees, hands behind his head. The American demanded to know where the minefields were located. The prisoner replied with his name rank and serial number. "Where are the damn minefields?", the officer shouted. With an arrogant look on his face the prisoner gave his name rank and serial number. The American fired his carbine between the German's knees. With a smirk on his face the German pointed to his crotch and said, "*Nichts hier.*" Then he pointed to his head and said, "*Hier.*" '

Slaughter commented, 'This convinced me we were fighting first-rate soldiers.'[56]

Mines caused a significant percentage of Allied men and *matériel* losses and caused the Allies to use large amounts of engineer resources. Fully one-quarter of all American troops landing in Normandy were engineers. Owing to the crust-like nature of the Atlantic Wall, once penetrated the Allies were able to move inland with relative ease. Had the Germans been able to lay minefields in sufficient depth the invasion would certainly have been more keenly fought. Ultimately the Germans were simply overwhelmed by a superior force willing to press home the attack.

The Campaign for North-west Europe

As the Allies pushed across north-west Europe the shortcomings in their mine-clearance equipment started to become apparent. Flails were good on hard ground but frequently got bogged down off the road and soft ground absorbed the impact of the chains. Rollers had mobility problems too and could not sustain repeated blasts. Explosive ropes broke, got caught in cross-winds or trees and failed to remove all the mines. All the new methods had their merits too, but it was quickly apparent that no panacea had been found.

To add to the problems, the Germans started to use increasing quantities of wooden, glass, clay and plastic mines. These were impossible to locate using the detectors of the day and caused many problems. Attempting to bridge the Ruhr in north-west Germany, the 246th Engineer Combat Battalion swept the approach for mines but their detectors did not find the plastic *Topf* mines that had been buried there. The undiscovered mines destroyed a wrecker, two tractors and two dump trucks and the engineers spent six hours prodding the entire area before progress could resume.[57]

An American account of the advance into Germany recalled that:

'Particularly disturbing were nests of non-metallic, anti-personnel *Schu* and anti-tank *Topf* mines, neither of which responded to ordinary mine detection devices . . . the worst losses occurred when the 117th Infantry's Company F stumbled into an anti-personnel minefield on the western fringe of Mariadorf. German shelling forced abandonment of all attempts to extricate the company until nightfall. The company lost sixty men.'[58]

As a result of these difficulties the British in particular started to use dogs (discussed more fully in Chapter 5) to hunt for mines and also developed a compressed-air jet for route clearance operations. A compressor was mounted on a truck with two air jets attached to long hoses. A sapper operated each jet in front of the truck, swinging it across a track, blasting away loose soil and thus exposing any mines. The technique was useful for checking recently mined roads out of combat areas, but otherwise had limited application.

During the campaign the Germans became adept at tricking troops into minefields. Of an incident in France on 26 July 1944 Lieutenant Miller wrote in his diary, 'I saw more dead Americans today than I have since D-Day. The Germans are planting mustard pot mines (S mines) in the ditches and then, when they shell the roads, the Doughboys jump in the ditches and blow themselves up.'[59]

Throughout the campaign mines inhibited the Allies and returned a steady stream of casualties. British and American tank losses to mines were 22.1 and 19 per cent of their total losses, respectively. British records also indicate at least twenty-two occasions when there were delays due to minefields, costing on average, 15.3 hours per event.[60]

Conclusions

During the Second World War the landmine did indeed become a 'new form of warfare'. In contrast to their desultory use in the century before 1939, mines rapidly became a standard feature of the battlefield. Originally employed to counter tanks, mines rapidly demonstrated a utility beyond the casualties they inflicted. In the battle of materials, the *Materialschlacht*, they provided economy for the defender and imposed attrition upon the attacker. They slowed down the pace of battle and smothered attempts at blitzkrieg. Methods of countering the mine were never entirely satisfactory and the initiative always remained with the defender. Of all the hazards of war the mine was the most insidious and the most feared, providing a disturbing psychological dimension. Soldiers could fight against all other weapons, but the unseen, passive mine defied aggression. The multifaceted effects of mines demonstrated during the greatest of wars ensured that they would remain an integral part of war in the future.

References and Notes

1. War Office (1952), p. 330.
2. Pakenham-Walsh, Vol.VIII, p. 139.
3. Ibid., Vol.X, p. 288.
4. Hartcup, pp. 195–6.
5. Donovan and Moat, p. 1.
6. Orpen and Martin, Vol.2, p. 45.
7. Stiff, p. 19.
8. Ibid., p. 88.
9. Majdalany, *Battle of El Alamein*, p. 146.
10. Young, p. 193.
11. Engineer Agency for Resource Inventories, Vol.3, p. 15.
12. War Office (1952), p. 333.
13. Liddell Hart, *Rommel Papers*, p. 195.

14. War Office (1952), p. 334.
15. Stiff, p. 23.
16. Quoted in Hamilton, pp. 793–4.
17. Royal School of Military Engineering [?], 'Engineer Lessons (First Army) from the North African Campaign, May 41– May 43, p. 10 [copy in Royal Engineers Library].
18. Stiff, p. 26.
19. Moore, p. 197.
20. Beck *et al.*, p. 100.
21. 'Nitebar', p. 67.
22. War Office (1952), p. 338.
23. Ibid., pp. 336–7.
24. H.G. Hee, quoted in Donovan and Moat, p. 7.
25. Keegan, p. 71.
26. Engineer Agency for Resource Inventories, Vol.18, p. 3.
27. Zatylkin, p. 23.
28. Quoted in Liddell Hart, *Red Army*, p. 135.
29. Col.-Gen. A. Tsirlin, *The Battle of Kursk* (Moscow: Progress Publishers, 1974), p. 220.
30. Zatylkin, p. 19.
31. Dixon and Heilbrunn, p. 143.
32. Liddell Hart, *Rommel Papers*, p. 452.
33. Engineer Agency for Resource Inventories, Vol.18, p. 93.
34. Liddell Hart, *Red Army*, p. 372.
35. Ibid., p. 372.
36. Liddell Hart, *Rommel Papers*, p. 452.
37. Halloran, p. 115.
38. Beck *et al.*, p. 181.
39. Doubler, p. 112.
40. Beck *et al.*, p. 181.
41. McLaughlin-Green *et al.*, p. 390.
42. Beck *et al.*, p. 197.
43. Ibid., p. 198.
44. H.G. Hee, quoted in Donovan and Moat, p. 7.
45. Belote and Belote, p. 224.
46. H.G. Hee, quoted in Donovan and Moat, p. 7.
47. Golino and Grimaldi, p. 1.
48. Quoted in Ambrose, p. 588.
49. Liddell Hart, *Rommel Papers*, p. 457.
50. McLaughlin-Green *et al.*, pp. 391–2.
51. War Department (1944).
52. Ambrose, pp. 220–2.
53. Ibid., pp. 281–2.

54. Ibid., p. 462.
55. Ibid., p. 292.
56. J. Slaughter, quoted in Ambrose, p. 460.
57. Beck *et al.*, p. 128.
58. McDonald, p. 500.
59. Quoted in Hoyt, p. 452.
60. Donovan and Moat, pp. A2–B1.

Chapter 5

Clearing Mines after the Second World War

On 7 May 1945 Germany surrendered, ending the war in Europe. The previous six years had been the greatest period of death and destruction ever experienced in man's history. Much of Europe lay in ruins, millions of people were displaced, economies were shattered, urban areas were destroyed, and the debris of war lay everywhere. Among the debris lay over a hundred million mines, still active but largely unseen. Minefields were often indistinguishable from safe areas and, unable to recognize the end of hostilities, they started to claim civilian lives. Mines had shifted with the movement of soil, vegetation had grown over many areas and records of their locations were not always available. Clearing minefields during the chaotic post-war period was clearly going to be a monumental undertaking, but amid so many other priorities the task was generally undertaken pragmatically.

While peacetime mine clearance was not as hazardous as it was in combat, it still ranked high among dangerous occupations. Deminers could expect on average to take one casualty for every 3,200 mines cleared. During the war some attempts had been made to clear redundant minefields. In May 1943 the US 20th Engineer Regiment was ordered to clear the Sedjenane Valley in Tunisia, ultimately removing over 200,000 mines. It was clearly an unpopular decision:

'Why? Virtually everyone objected. Why? The fields had no military value; they were only worked by Arabs. Removing mines was enormously difficult and dangerous, thousands of mines in thick bush and scrub that would only be trod on by Arabs and their beasts. Almost every day there were casualties . . . Seven officers and nineteen men killed because someone thought it was a good idea to clear the Sedjenane and nobody stopped it.'[1]

The account indicates not only the risks in mine clearance but the manner in which attitudes towards civilian casualties have changed in the past half century.

The US 10th Engineer Combat Battalion also took heavy casualties during the clearance of the Formia-Gaeta area, north of Naples in 1944. A sixteen-day operation to clear 20,000 mines resulted in fifteen fatalities and forty-two injuries.[2] There were a variety of motives for conducting out of combat clearance, including the need to occupy the area, concern for civilian casualties, live training, or the requirement to obtain mines for re-use. In general, though, such operations were rare as all resources were directed to defeating the enemy rather than to restoring the environment.

The Clearing of the British Beaches

The last chapter outlined the mining of beaches in southern England and showed how the requirement to move certain minefields provided the British with their first experience of mine clearing. After the war 350,000 mines in about two thousand individual fields needed to be cleared. The location of many of them had not been recorded and a questionnaire was issued to coastal inhabitants asking if they knew of the presence of any minefields. The Prime Minister C.R. Attlee replied to a parliamentary question about mines on 17 October 1945, 'The location of mines is a difficult problem, particularly as many have been shifted by tides and soil movements . . . I am afraid that complete clearance might take some time.' Mr Attlee was right, by February 1948 338,500 mines had been cleared but full clearance was not complete until 1958 and the last mined beach, at Trimmingham in Norfolk, was not opened to the public until 1972.

Apart for the inconvenience of having large areas of the coast off limits, the minefields returned a steady stream of civilian casualties, including a number of children. One of the earliest incidents was in August 1942 when two teenagers, Robert Adams and Frank Smith, went into a minefield 'near a certain foreshore' to collect a ball they were playing with. Smith was killed and Adams was injured. After the war a case was brought against the soldier responsible for the minefield on the premise that it was poorly marked and insufficiently guarded. The defendant claimed that the children had ignored the danger signs, that the minefield was on private property and therefore the children were trespassing and, finally, that the injuries were war injuries. The case was dismissed.[3]

The beach mines even proved lethal to children born after they had been laid. In one of the worst incidents, five schoolboys aged between eleven and thirteen, were killed when playing with a mine they discovered on the beach at Swanage in Dorset. The beach had been swept twice using detectors and had been open to the public since 1950. At the inquiry Major Hartley, Royal Engineers, claimed in a contradictory statement, 'The beach is perfectly safe, but I could not be certain that mines would not be washed up again.' Death by misadventure was recorded.[4]

The clearing of the beaches was undertaken by the Royal Engineers and Ukrainian prisoners of war.[5] The methods of finding mines were: visual; 4A (Polish) detectors – capable of finding a B Type C mine at up to 2.5ft; ERA (Electronic Research Agency) deep locators – operated by two men and capable of finding a B type C at up to 5ft; armoured bulldozers – used for removing top layers of sand before a second check with detectors and a high-pressure water jet. The last was a peacetime innovation developed in response to the problem of sand shifting and burying mines too deep to be detected. The water jet was mounted on an armoured Bren-gun carrier and a Leyland pump drew water from the sea delivering 100,000gall/hr at 150–200lb/sq. in through an 8in hose. The water washed away the sand and exposed mines which could be destroyed *in situ*.[6] Another peacetime innovation was the use of flame throwers to clear vegetation from inland minefields.

Despite these cautious methods, casualties were high, between 1945 and 1957 155 deminers were killed and a further 55 injured.[7] In recognition of their service and acknowledging bomb and mine clearance duties performed between 1945 and 1949, a clasp to the General Service Medal was awarded to those engaged on operations for 180 days. This was the first campaign medal to be issued for service in the United Kingdom. Some involved in the operation were decorated for bravery: in 1953 the George Medal was awarded to Captain Hough and the British Empire Medal to Warrant Officer Thomas, both of the Royal Engineers, for their attempts to rescue two of their colleagues who had been blown up on Mundesley beach.

Mine-clearance Dogs

In 1940 an experimental school was established in Britain to explore the potential of dogs for a variety of military tasks, such as guarding, patrolling and delivering messages. After initial successes it was decided early in 1944 to try and employ the dogs' remarkable olfactory senses to detect mines.

The most obedient and responsive dogs were trained to identify explosive scents and to ignore distractions including 'pinioned rabbits, sheep, game, lumps of meat and even "in season" bitches'. After meeting the required standards the dogs, which included crossbreeds, Alsatians, retrievers and collies, were organized into four platoons, each with four sections of four.[8]

Between July 1944 and November 1945 the four dog platoons were employed in north-west Europe with the British and the Canadian Army. However, their employment was generally limited to the finding of isolated explosive items since it was felt that minefield smells were too confusing for them. The dogs were employed for checking railways and electricity power lines and for proving that ground was clear. No.2 Dog Platoon, Royal Engineers operating in Holland in 1945 cleared 153 miles of railway and 73 miles of power line. They located twenty-nine mines but had two accidents involving one dog and two handlers.[9] One of the dog platoon commanders, Captain J. R. Davison, put the efforts of the dogs into perspective:

'The value of the mine clearing dog cannot be assessed by the number of mines located with his aid ... His real value,

87

however, was the saving of time and of labour, and in the saving of lives of both soldiers and civilians. Quite incidently in the course of his daily duties he often found very few mines over areas which, but for his aid, might have remained unchecked for a long time, used at great risk or else unused at great economic cost.'[10]

Attempts were made to use dogs to locate mines on the beaches of Britain but shifting sands buried many of the mines too deep for their discovery. A small number of mine-clearance dogs were retained within the Army for some years after the war. At a Royal Engineers' display at Hawley in May 1950 they demonstrated their skills before a fascinated audience and a correspondent from *The Times* wrote of them, 'No one seems yet to know what canine sense comes into play . . . but long experience of finding buried bones may have something to do with it.'

Prisoners of War as Mine Deminers

For the victors, German prisoners of war (PoWs) were the obvious resource to use in clearing mines. After all, the majority of mines had been laid by the Germans and it was they who had started the war, causing so much misery. This matter-of-fact approach foundered upon the humane and intelligent stance of the International Committee of the Red Cross (ICRC) and the fledgling United Nations. The ICRC asserted that the use of PoWs for mine clearance was implicitly forbidden under the terms of the Geneva Convention of 1929 which stated that they could not be employed on 'dangerous' work.[11] As few mines had been used in previous wars no specific clause existed about using PoWs for clearance. It was argued that mine clearance could not be classified as 'dangerous' because the work was entrusted to soldiers who had received previous training. It was a fine argument; training reduced the risks but certainly did not eliminate them. Eventually the situation was resolved by postponing an official judgment until clearance was complete and in August 1949 the Geneva Convention closed the legal loophole and expressly forbade the use of PoWs for this purpose.

88

On 13 May 1945 the Prefect of L'Aube at the village of Bucheres in France, which had been destroyed in reprisals by the German SS, spoke to newly-formed PoW mine clearance teams, 'The guilty party is not Hitler alone, but all his accomplices, that is to say, the whole of Germany. As for you, there is nothing more for you to do other than to remake your souls, change your attitude, repair the damage you have done, and work.'[12] The French employed up to 49,000 PoWs on mine clearance (alongside around 3,000 French civilians plus military units) and a further 450,000 on other agricultural, mining and reconstruction work. Thousands of other PoWs were employed on mine clearance and other tasks throughout Europe and the Soviet Union. In Germany the allocation of deminers was co-ordinated through the *Dienstgruppen* (Labour Service Corps) and supervised by the occupying armies.

The life of a PoW deminer must have been miserable. Living in poor conditions with meagre rations, uncertain when he would return home, or what he would return home to, and with the constant humiliation and threat of retribution from his former enemies. The work was, of course, dangerous, between 8 and 17.5 per cent of all such mine clearers were killed or injured in the period 1945–46.[13]

The work progressed remarkably quickly. This was because of the excellent plans made by the German army (which the PoWs had every reason to hand over), the belief that they could return home once the task was complete and especially the large number of men put to work. The prisoners were also given a strong incentive to ensure that all mines were removed; they were required to march, shoulder to shoulder, across any area that they cleared.[14] This method of checking cleared ground appears barbaric to liberal society in the Western world today, but, in reality, marching across cleared minefields is more of a symbolic gesture. During the course of normal clearance operations almost every square foot is walked upon; marching across cleared minefields is an efficient way of transmitting confidence to the civilian population who subsequently use the area.

In the Netherlands civilians anxious to restore their land commenced clearance operations as soon as their country was liberated. Their efforts proved 'not very fruitful' and they suffered

89

twenty-six fatalities and twenty-three injuries.[15] In July 1945 the German 25th Army was ordered to complete the task under Canadian supervision. The German Engineer 'Draeger' Brigade, consisting of 104 officers and 3,244 men cleared 247sq. km of the coast and 39.5sq. km between Nijmegen and Arnhem in about eight months. During this period they cleared 1,079,857 mines and sustained 179 fatalities and 384 injuries.[16] A list of mines cleared by the Brigade is shown in the accompanying table.

A *Dienstgruppen* team cleared a 969sq. km area of the German border around Aachen of around 760,000 mines. The task took two years, involving up to 1,340 men of whom 108 were killed and 112 were injured.[17] In France around 13 million mines were cleared between 1945 and 1946,[18] with 2,217 killed and 3,630 injured in the process. In two months 300 PoWs cleared 67,000 mines from Guernsey with 8 killed and 14 injured.[19]

Type of mine	Number lifted	Percentage of total
Teller, 29,35,42,43, *Topf*	200,456	18.5
Holzmine 42	87,173	8.1
Riegel 43	40,722	3.8
British Mk 3, 4, 5	12,463	1.1
US AT	8,497	0.8
French AT	83,179	7.7
S mine 35, 44	127,591	11.8
Schu 42	229,431	21.2
Stock	15,748	1.5
'AP German'	43,769	4.1
Shells and ordnance	76,665	7.1
Improvised mines	29,989	2.8
French S150, S200 AP	88,406	8.2
British shrapnel	3,570	0.3
Others	32,199	3.0
Total	1,079,858	100.0

The clearance of the Soviet Union after the war was considered part of the heroic national effort. Not only were PoW and Soviet military units employed on clearance:

'Volunteer groups came forward in the villages, were given instruction in demining and then, under the direction of experienced sappers, probed every yard of ground, every bush and every riverbank. These volunteer groups were joined not only by the young folk and women, but also old peasants who had once served in the Russian Army.'[20]

After the war 58.5 million mines and 122 million items of unexploded munitions were removed from Soviet soil, including half a million items that were located by dogs. The efforts of Soviet deminers and the lingering hazards of mines were expressed in the poem 'Duel' by Yuri Melnikov written in 1972:

> 'Back from the front lines
> We came home long ago
> But even now
> In the sand and clay
> Lie undetonated mines
> From this hard war
>
> Young soldiers bend over war's remains
> With scalpels they bend down
> In the cold and the wet
> Near homes and in the aspen grove
> They have been fighting a fearless duel'

By 1948 more than 90 per cent of the clearance work in Europe was complete and most of the PoWs had returned home. The remainder of the work was carried out over a period of decades by much smaller national contingents. The residue were left because their locations were unknown, the areas were not a high priority or because they were considered too difficult to clear. In Poland from 1945 to 1947 14,392,000 mines were cleared and a further 502,000 between 1948 and 1982. North Africa, without the benefit of a large PoW population, was largely left to suffer the consequences of hosting a battle it did not invite. North Africa especially, but also parts of Europe, continue to unearth mines (along with other items of explosive ordnance) for half a century after the war (see Addendum to this chapter).

91

Methods of Clearance

While advances in combat breaching had been made during the war, mechanical and explosive clearance had little place in peacetime operations. Combat breaching was (and remains) an expedient method of rapidly getting from one side of a minefield to the other, speed and protection being the key requirements. The rate of clearance of combat breaching was too low for peacetime requirements and, besides, flails which offered the highest rate of clearance had too many limitations for peacetime demining. The simple fact is that demining can be quick or it can be thorough, it cannot be both. However, in Poland mechanical methods were employed to check the ground after manual demining, cleared land was thoroughly ploughed by a sapper who would watch for any further mines as the soil was turned. Apart from this form of quality control mechanical clearance was rarely used.

Although there were some innovative techniques employed on the beaches of Britain, most mine clearance was undertaken by the use of simple prodders and electronic detectors. The presence of non-metallic mines frequently meant that deminers more generally relied on prodding. Although prodding was an extremely slow method of clearance, if a plan were available the rate of clearance could be quite rapid. In Holland, a combination of good records and sandy soil allowed clearance rates of around 27,400sq. m per man per week; with poor records and difficult soil the rate dropped to 8,800sq. m per man per week. Most mines were examined for booby traps and then disarmed but suspect mines were destroyed *in situ*. This was achieved by detonating a small charge next to the mine, by dragging a heavy weight across it, or by pulling the trip wire with a hook and line.

The Impact on Civilians

Civilians generally fled combat areas and often returned home after the fighting to discover their homes wrecked and large areas of land off-limits because of mines and other ordnance. In Libya

87 per cent of range land and 9 per cent of cereal land was rendered unusable by the presence of mines. As late as 1980 37 per cent of range land remained unusable. This had a major effect on agricultural production and the economy as a whole. In addition to the large number of civilian casualties, the loss of livestock due to mines averaged more than 3,000 animals per year in the four decades following the end of the war.[22]

In Poland about 2 per cent of the country was heavily mined by Soviet and German forces and a much larger proportion had a smaller degree of contamination – from seventy-eight different types of mine. In the first five years after the war agricultural production was inhibited by approximately 10 per cent. In the early post-war years civilian casualties from mines and other ordnance averaged in excess of 900 a year, with a total of 4,094 killed and 8,774 wounded by 1981. A nationwide programme of public education on explosive remnants was instituted to ameliorate the situation but accidents, particularly involving curious children, continued. In France between 1944 and 1948 at least 520 civilians were killed and 821 were injured in accidents involving landmines.[23]

Conclusion

Mines influenced many aspects of post-war life, slowing reconstruction, reducing agricultural production and returning a steady stream of casualties. In war-ravaged countries mines were only one of many obstacles to the restoration of normality, their effects were significant but not desperate. The fact that only around 10 per cent of the total PoW workforce was employed on mine clearance indicates that there were plenty of other higher-priority, labour-intensive tasks. The civilian casualties caused by mines in the post-war period were tragic but generally accepted phlegmatically by the public. Many countries had lost hundreds of thousands of civilians during the war itself and were inured to suffering. Consequently the problem of mines did not become a controversial topic for public debate. Perhaps the most remarkable aspect of post-war clearance was the speed with which it was achieved. By applying a large amount of mostly PoW labour the clearance of around 90 million mines was achieved within two years of the cessation of hostilities.

References and Notes

1. Hoyt, pp. 197–8.
2. Beck *et al.*, p. 182.
3. *The Times*, 2 April 1946.
4. Ibid., 14 May 1955.
5. Unable or unwilling to return home after their release, many of the Ukrainians elected to remain in Britain as civilian mine and munition clearers; as late as 1962 there were still 113 of them working on such projects.
6. Hough, pp. 257–65.
7. McBean, pp. 3–4.
8. Vesey-Fitzgerald, pp. 188–9.
9. Military Operational Research Unit. Report No.7, p. 8.
10. Quoted in Vesey-Fitzgerald, p. 190.
11. A similar debate about the use of Confederate troops to clear mines was mentioned in Chapter 1.
12. Quoted in Voldman, p. 100.
13. Extracted from records of PoW clearance in France, the Netherlands, Guernsey and Germany.
14. Military Operational Research Unit, p. 6.
15. *History of the Corps of Royal Engineers*, Vol.VII, p. 556.
16. Ibid., pp. 1–17.
17. HQ, 2nd British Infantry Division, *Report on Operation TAPPET*, pp. 1–7.
18. B.A. Molski and J. Pajak in Westing, p. 27.
19. Beckingham, p. 213.
20. Engineer Agency for Resource Inventories, Vol.18, p. 2.
21. Quoted in Zatylkin, p. 24.
22. Khairi Sgaier in Westing, pp. 33–7.
23. Quoted in Voldman, p. 149.

Addendum

Estimates of Mines Cleared and Casualties Sustained during Clearance Operations after World War Two

Country/Area	Period	Millions of mines cleared	Deminers killed	Deminers injured	Total casualties	Mines cleared per casualty	Remarks
Austria	45–75	0.046	18	23	41	1,122	
Belgium	45–46	0.4	–	286	286	1,398	
Denmark	45–47	0.75	190	250	440	1,704	
England	44–57	0.35	155	55	210	1,666	
Finland	45–76	0.066	–	–	–	–	No casualty data available
France	45–45	13.0	2,127	3,630	5,757	2,258	
Germany	45–47	0.76	108	113	221	3,439	Operation TAPPET only
Guernsey	45	0.067	8	14	22	4,786	
Netherlands	45–46	1.08	205	407	613	1,762	
Italy	45–46	3.0	–	–	1,100	2,727	Figures are approximate
North Africa	43–90	estd 1.0	–	–	estd 600	1,667	
Norway	45–47	0.75	192	252	444	1,689	
Poland	45–56	14.76	404	571	975	15,138	Casualty figures extrapolated
USSR	45–46	58.5	–	–	–	–	No casualty data available
Average						3,279	
Total		94.53					

Notes

1. Total number of mines laid in period 1939–45 was probably in the region of 110 mill., broken down thus: Germany 35 mill., Soviet Union 67 mill., British and Americans 3 mill., others 5 mill. The remaining mines were either cleared over a longer period, functioned as designed or remain in place.
2. Casualty figures are probably underestimates; total number of casualties from the clearance operations was probably in the region of 40,000, plus an unknown number of civilians.
3. Accurate figures for the Balkans, Greece, the Pacific and other areas are not available.
4. Sources include Operational Clearance Reports. Westing, Voldman, Pakenham Walsh, Zatylkin, Beckingham and *Sunday Telegraph*.

Chapter 6

Limited War and Technical Improvements

The Second World War was a period of unprecedented advances in military technology. The war marked the start of the modern arms race, a race that diminished slightly in intensity upon the cessation of hostilities, but not in breadth nor scale. In 1939 the widespread employment of mines was virtually unknown, but by 1945 they were an important component of defence for all the major armies and over a hundred different types of mine had been used in combat. Mine warfare would never again be contemplated with derision as it had in the 1930s. The Second World War was in many ways the climax of mine warfare, the experience of mines since then has been limited but in general it has confirmed their 'Importance as major anti-armour and anti-personnel weapons which cause casualties, affect morale and reduce mobility.'[1]

The design of mines since 1945 has concentrated on five criteria: effectiveness, size, detectability, logistic effort, and speed of laying. The modern industrial age has witnessed considerable refinements in synthetic materials, electronics and production techniques, all of which could contribute to the development of mines. For the first time they were not the by-product of combat requirements alone but also the result of military–industrial innovation. Rapid technological advance resulted in rapid obsolescence and by the 1990s over six hundred types of mine had been produced. Progress in mine countermeasures was not as rapid and the clearance techniques of 1945 were still employed five decades later with minimal modification. The limited progress in counter-measures was in part a reflection of the lack of investment in that area, but more an indication of the intrinsic difficulty of locating buried ordnance, a problem which has defied easy solution to this day.

Each decade since 1945 has been characterized by different progressions. In broad terms, the 1950s saw an assimilation of the German methods of mining; the 1960s, the advent of offensive mining by guerrilla armies and the proliferation of plastic mines; the 1970s, the introduction of scatterable mines; and the 1980s and the 1990s, electronic fuzes and the use of artillery and supersonic aircraft to deliver mines. This chapter describes the use of mines in a number of wars during these years and outlines the parallel technological progress.

The Korean War

The Korean War of 1950–54 pitched United Nations forces and South Korea against North Korea and China. It offered the first widespread opportunity for the lessons of World War Two to be applied, but the UN forces frequently appeared slow at putting the lessons into practice. The war opened with a surprise invasion of the South in June 1950. UN forces under American leadership arrived in August and reversed North Korean gains. This precipitated a Chinese invasion and the UN withdrew to the 38th parallel where the front was eventually stabilized.

Both sides used mines to cover their withdrawals and to enhance defences. The mountainous terrain greatly restricted vehicular movement (as it had in Italy and the Pacific islands) and the valleys and passes were obvious places in which to lay mines. That terrain greatly influenced minelaying was clear from the statistics; in Korea 80 mines were laid per tank casualty compared with 2,000 per tank casualty in north-west Europe and 38 per cent of tank casualties were due to mines.[2] Of American troop casualties, mines accounted for 1.65 per cent of those killed and 3.32 per cent of those wounded.[3]

At the outset of the war the South Koreans had no concept of mine warfare. Major Richard Crawford of the Korean Military

Advisory Group observed, 'The necessity for some type of land-mine was becoming increasingly apparent as more enemy armour came in. At the outset we had no source of anti-tank mines.' The situation was soon rectified with the United States supplying their M6 mine (2.5 million of these mines were manufactured in 1944 but they arrived too late to be used in the war). During the initial invasion the South Koreans developed their own style of mine warfare. Soldiers would strap explosives to their bodies and hurl themselves at enemy tanks. Having made contact they would pull the fuze and 'certainly join their honorable ancestors'. After a few days the South Koreans admitted to running short of volunteers.[4]

They also used mines in another, similarly brave but not quite so suicidal a manner. As four Chinese tanks approached Ham-hung, an American military advisor recalled, 'Two of my ROK engineers each ran twice across the road dropping M6 mines in the path of the tanks. All four enemy tanks were knocked out and the attack was stopped.'[5] This tactic gave rise to the require-ment for a mine which could attack a tank from the side of a road without soldiers having to take the extreme risk of running in front of enemy tanks. The Germans had already demonstrated the concept in their *Panzerfaust* off-route mine and this was copied by the USA in the M24 system. This incorporated a rocket with a shaped charge warhead which was launched horizontally from its concealed position at the side of a route when a tank crossed an activating wire.

After the arrival of UN forces mines were used more conven-tionally but the marking, recording and guarding of minefields by them was generally poor, as an American officer remarked:

'I have seen a great number of American tanks and trucks destroyed by our own mines. Not all of these were in minefields laid by Americans. A large percentage of the mines that destroyed our vehicles and killed our troops had been relaid by the enemy . . . American mine warfare doctrine is sound, but after the Eighth Army had shipped 120,000 mines to units, only 20,000 were recorded or on hand. The remaining 100,000 were either abandoned or buried! . . . Failure to record minefields was a serious problem in Korea.'[6]

In one incident Australian forces suffered fifty casualties when they 'unwittingly entered an unmarked, unrecorded minefield which the Canadians had laid around an outpost position.'[7] After the war an official American account noted that, 'One of the tragic losses of Korea were [*sic*] the casualties inflicted on UN troops by UN-laid minefields that were unrecorded.'[8]

The situation was undoubtedly caused by lack of mine warfare training, a common theme since mines were first introduced. The problem with such training is threefold: first, it is extremely tedious and unfulfilling to lay training mines; secondly, on manoeuvres armour and infantry have a tendency to simply disregard minefields, and, lastly, minelaying appears so simple and repetitive that it is often felt that little training is required. As a consequence engineers tend to engage in more interesting training such as bridging and demolitions and other arms become complacent about the mine threat. Once in combat, troops have to learn by hard experience the lessons that should have been taught in a less hostile environment. Field Marshal Sir Nigel Bagnall explained the difference between mine warfare training and practice: 'Given some live mines . . . dash would be replaced by caution, determination by prudence and contempt by a healthy respect. The psychological effect of mines is of considerable importance.'[9]

When used thoughtfully mines proved effective at disrupting the enemy. Defensive positions around Naktong were seeded with anti-personnel mines and, regarding one position, an American officer claimed that 'defended anti-personnel fields . . . accounted for 113 enemy casualties in a two-hour night attack.'[10] The Chinese and the North Koreans adopted Soviet doctrine and threw men at minefields regardless of casualties. While minefields were not always capable of stopping this form of attack, they certainly reduced the number of men who reached their objective. The tactic also prompted the US military to call for 'A light anti-personnel mine that is a guaranteed casualty producer, a sort of counterpart to the Red Schu that would be more adaptable than the Bouncing Betty.'[11] (The latter was the nickname for the M16 bounding fragmentation mine.)

After the war, the Americans produced the M14 pressure mine and the M18 Claymore directional fragmentation mine to fill the gap in capabilities. The M14 was a tiny (40mm high and 56mm in diameter) minimum metal mine known as the 'toe popper'. The Claymore was particularly useful at stopping human wave-tactics. It could be detonated by trip wire or an electric command wire and hurled hundreds of steel ball bearings into a 60-degree arc to a lethal range of 50m. Claymore-type mines have since become a standard feature in all armies of the world.

The British had updated their mines immediately before the Korean War. Their new anti-personnel mine – the No.6 – was probably the most advanced of its day when it was introduced in 1948. Nicknamed the 'carrot mine', it was indeed shaped like a carrot, its slender form designed to make detection by prodder difficult and its plastic construction provided an effective counter to metal detectors. The new anti-tank mine – the Mark 7 – was brought into service in 1950. With 8.89kg (19.6lb) of explosive it was the largest mine of the period, designed to cut the heaviest tank tracks with half the mine covered. Furthermore, its fuse could be set to detonate the mine after the second impulse, making it effective against explosive clearance methods or rollers.

On occasions mines were used to provide economies in defence. The South Korean 6th Division defending Sinnyong had to occupy an extremely long, irregularly shaped front but, 'Shrewd use of mines allowed the Division to straighten its line and shift a maximum number of troops to the offensive.'[12] The use of mines on this front also proved extremely effective: at Yodok-tong a North Korean infantry company ran into the minefield:

'Almost the entire company got into the first belt of mines (mostly M3s[13]) before they hit the first trip wire and realized their predicament. Mines exploded and men screamed. The attackers turned in panic only to kick up more trip wires. The whole affair lasted scarcely five minutes, yet we estimated a hundred casualties.'[14]

During the same battle anti-tank mines were planted in the road behind advancing North Korean tanks. The leading tank was knocked out by bazooka fire and the first of the retreating tanks ran into the mines, trapping nine others in a valley which were then destroyed by air strikes.

17. A British sapper
    uncarths a German
    plastic *Topf* mine;
    the Germans
    surrounded these
    with radioactive
    sand to enable them
    to be located by
    Geiger counter.
    Photo: *Royal
    Engineers*

18. British troops
    wearing improvised
    protective kit search
    for mines in the
    Netherlands in
    1944. Photo: *IWM*

19. Compressed air being used to find and uncover a *Tellermine 42* in Belgium; the technique had few applications and was suitable only for locating recently buried mines away from the battlefield. Photo: *IWM*

20. Japanese forces placed horned beach mines below the waterline to disrupt amphibious landings in the Pacific Campaign; these are awaiting destruction. Photo: *Royal Engineers*

21. Many German prisoners of war were used after the war to clear minefields; to ensure that they had been thorough and to assure the local population the PoWs were marched through the areas they had cleared. Photo: *IWM*

22. The Royal Engineers used dogs to clear railway lines in the Netherlands after the war; dogs could locate isolated mines but became confused by multiple scents in dense minefields. Photo: *Royal Engineers*

23. Water jets were used on some British beaches to find the many mines laid in expectation of a German invasion. Photo: *Royal Engineers*

24. Since the beginning of the Second World War over 600 types of mine have been produced world-wide. Photo: *Mike Croll*

25. The South African Buffel mine-protected vehicle; damage to it and harm to
its occupants are minimized by the V-shaped hull. Photo: *Mike Croll*

26. A Barmine about to be
buried; substantial
savings in manpower
result from mechanical
laying. Photo: *Bovington
Tank Museum*

27. The Skorpian scatterable mine system mounted on an Alvis Stormer armoured vehicle in service with the British Army during the Gulf War; this is capable of laying a minefield in seconds. Photo: *Bovington Tank Museum*

28. An Aardvark flail clearing mines in support of humanitarian operations in Afghanistan. Photo: *Aardvark Clear Mine Ltd*

29. A UN deminer in Mozambique; manual clearance is still the most effective method of removing mines in spite of its evident drawbacks; note how the vegetation is cleared to allow the detector head to work close to the ground. Photo: *Mike Croll*

30. The results of treading on an anti-personnel mine. Photo: *Elizabeth Sheehan*

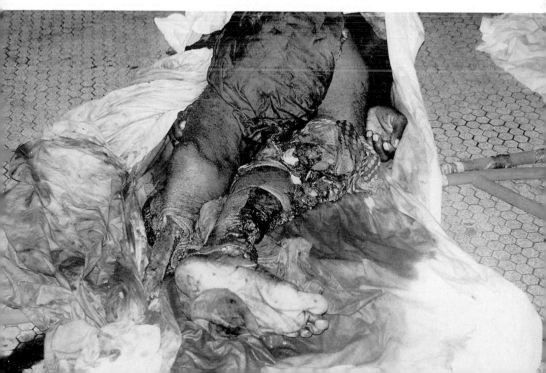

31. Amputees in a Mozambican prosthetic clinic. Photo: *Elizabeth Sheehan*

32. Villagers in Namiaroi distric
Mozambique excavate a roa
to check for mines: a simple
albeit labour-intensive syste
that has proved highly
effective in practice. Photo:
Nick Bateman

UN countermine tactics were essentially limited to manual methods – the educated eye and the sharp bayonet. As the North Koreans used principally wooden-cased mines – Soviet-made TMDs and PMD 6s[15] – the electronic detector was of limited effectiveness. A British officer remarked on discovering two PMD 6s with a prodder: 'The exceptional thing about [them] . . . was that we had actually found them without harm being done. I never heard of any others being found at the time except by claiming a target.'[16]

In the late 1940s the Americans had issued the AN/PRS-1 non-metallic mine detector but it never gained the confidence of the soldiers as the false alarm rate on stones and clods of soil was so high. Ploughs were again the mainstay of mechanized breaching; flails were not introduced until 1952 and the use of explosive hoses was inhibited by the terrain. Mine-walking shoes were tested during the war. These were essentially air-filled snow shoes designed to spread a man's weight below the threshold required to detonate a mine. Their use was extremely limited since they could still initiate trip wires and they were unwieldy in the difficult mountainous terrain. One new technique for dealing with undetectable wooden-cased mines was to excavate the road to the depth of a foot, thus exposing any buried mines. It was only suitable for out-of-combat areas and no mines were discovered using the technique. The British officer in charge of the project remarked that 'It was a pity that the Chinese could not be told how successful their few mines had been.'[17]

In general, the Korean War served to underline the lessons of the Second World War rather than to illuminate any new aspects. Where properly employed, mines provided significant benefits to the defender, but if used carelessly they become a hazard to everyone. However, to the United States the potential of the mine was clear, as a Field Manual written after the war explained:

'Mines are among the best artificial obstacles – they are portable, installed relatively easily, and constitute a hazard to the enemy; however, large scale employment of mines requires considerable time, manpower, and logistical effort. Mines delay and canalize enemy movement, lower the enemy's will to fight, and cause fear of sudden and unexpected casualties.'[18]

After the war, in addition to the M24 off-route mine and the new anti-personnel mines (the M14 and the Claymore), the US also produced the M21 anti-tank mine. Again this was based on earlier German mines and incorporated a Miznay-Shardin shaped charge and a tilt rod. The Miznay-Shardin shaped charge was a shallow dish of copper on top of the main explosive. On detonation, the copper plate forms a flat projectile which travels vertically at great speed and is capable of penetrating armour and causing a lethal over-pressure inside a tank. The tilt rod enables the mine to attack the full width of a tank and thus the M21 was not only lethal in its effect but fewer of them were required than of conventional, pressure-operated mines.

The new types of mine were versatile and complementary and heralded a new approach to mine warfare. The optimum density of minefields and the probability of tanks encountering the mines were carefully calculated and fields were designed to mathematical formulae as the accompanying graph indicates.

That the Americans had faith in the ability of mines to shape the defensive battle was clear when they laid a massive minefield across the 38th parallel in Korea in 1965 to deter or delay any future invasion.

The Vietnam War

The improvements in mine warfare capability in the late 1950s and the early 1960s were made not only in response to the Korean experience but also because it was felt that mines would play a major role in stopping Warsaw Pact forces in the event of a European war. However, the first operational deployment of the new mines was in Vietnam where the barrier minefield concept was of little use. In fact, it was the Americans there who found themselves on the receiving end of mine warfare. The Vietnam War seared the soul of the United States, which, for all its material and technical superiority, was unable to defeat its shadowy enemy. Part of the reason for the defeat lay in the inability to cope with the Vietcong's method of offensive mine warfare, which at times paralysed US forces. The Soviet Army first used the tactic behind German forces in 1943 but the Vietcong 'successfully

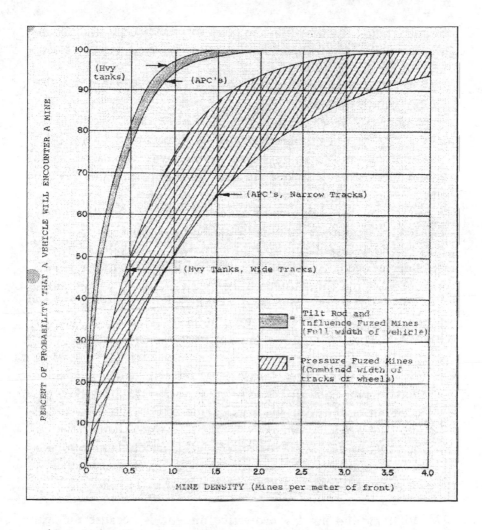

substituted mines for artillery'[19] and caused an unprecedented number of casualties and massive disruption.

The Vietcong's arsenal was considerably more limited than that of the United States. They had a small supply of imported anti-tank mines, including the Soviet-made TMD and TM 46, the East German plastic PM60, and the Chinese cast-iron No.4. For anti-personnel mines they used the Soviet PMD 6 and the new bakelite PMN. The latter replaced the PMD 6 as the main Soviet anti-personnel mine in the early 1960s; its main advantage was in the speed of laying. The PMD 6 consisted of a wooden case, explosive charge, detonator and fuse all of which were supplied separately, the mine being assembled in the field; the PMN with its bakelite case simply needed to have the detonator inserted and the safety pin removed.

At least a third of Vietcong mines were locally improvised devices, crudely manufactured in the field by the use of tin cans or bamboo tubes as containers and explosives chipped out of unexploded American munitions. An indication of their difficulty in obtaining and manufacturing mines was the widespread employment of *panji* spikes and the reintroduction to the battle-field of the caltrop – known in Vietnam as the 'crow's foot'.

To make up for their lack of resources, the Vietcong frequently resorted to 'stealing' from minefields. A senior officer stated, 'One must expect a guerrilla to lift mines because it provides him with a wonderful ordnance depot.'[20] An indication of the extent of this practice was that an estimated 16 per cent of American mine casualties and 50 per cent of total Australian casualties[21] were caused by American-manufactured mines. The US commander General Westmoreland described the most audacious theft:

'One ingenious project the Australians attempted had an unhappy ending. In an effort to preserve a portion of Phouy Tuy province, the Australians laid some 20,000 anti-personnel mines, but South Vietnamese militia that were charged with protecting the field failed to keep out VC [Vietcong] infiltrators. The VC removed roughly half the mines and used them for their own purposes throughout the province.'[22]

The Vietcong did not lay protective minefields because the war seldom developed any 'fronts' as in conventional wars. Instead, they took mines to the enemy, targeting roads and footpaths, a simple, but for the Americans, deadly tactic. The losses to mines were staggering. On Highway 19 east of Pleiku between January and March 1967, eighty-eight vehicles struck mines and a further twenty-seven mines were detected. From June 1969 to June 1970 in the northern III Corps tactical zone, 352 vehicles struck mines and a further 750 mines were detected. A study made between November 1968 and May 1969 showed that 73 per cent of all tank and 78 per cent of all armoured personnel carrier (APC) losses were due to mines.[23]

Offensive mining caused the Americans to 'clear almost the entire Vietnam road net every day' and many casualties occurred during these operations.[24] Ploughs were of limited use as they were very slow and also removed the top layers of roads, making them impassable to wheeled vehicles in wet conditions. A mine roller was introduced late in 1969 but it never gained widespread acceptance among the troops and only twenty-seven were issued.[25] Field trials with explosive-detecting dogs were conducted in 1969 and 1970. Several dogs were wounded during these trials and they missed around 16 per cent of mines, but it was concluded that they were suitable for supplementing other clearance methods.[26] Small numbers of dogs continued to be used but, again, the main method of detection was the educated eye and a sharp prodder assisted by an electronic detector. An informant programme was also organized with cash incentives offered to civilians in return for information about mine locations, but only 0.6 per cent of all mines found were recovered through this scheme.[27]

To thwart American counter-mine efforts, the Vietcong resorted to a variety of tactics, including spreading metal fragments across roads to slow detector teams. On other occasions they would dig holes at night and wait until they had been checked by clearance teams before removing the loose soil and burying a mine to catch following vehicles. To prevent the telltale 'dishing' on top of a buried mine, rice was placed in the hole to expand and balance the effect of the soil's settling. Many roads were paved to prevent mines from being dug into them, but again the Vietcong were able to counter this. They tunnelled under the road and jammed mines under short wooden props which transmitted sufficient pressure to cause detonation when a heavy vehicle rolled over them.

The most successful of American attempts to cope with offensive mining was to prevent the Vietcong from laying mines. Aggressive patrolling was instituted, artillery fire was directed at areas where mine incidents were common, ambushes were set up and ground-emplaced sensors to detect enemy movement were used. These tactics did reduce incidents but never eliminated them and mines were a severe irritation throughout the war.

Armoured crews became increasingly nervous about mines. A

mine blast generally shattered a tank's running gear but rarely seriously injured the crew; however, in 1969 one of the first of the new Sheridan tanks hit a mine which ruptured the hull, ignited the ammunition and killed the crew. Armoured personnel carriers were especially vulnerable to mines. The occupants always wore helmets and flak jackets and laid sand bags and ration boxes on the floor to lesson the effects of a blast. Soldiers of the 1st Squadron, 1st Cavalry placed so many sandbags in their M113s, the standard US armoured personnel carrier, that they broke fourteen transmissions in the space of forty-five days through overloading. Most soldiers rode on top of their vehicles 'feeling it was better to get blown off the top than to be blown up inside'. [28] In 1970 belly-armour kits for M113s and Sheridans was issued to prevent blast rupture. This increased confidence but troops continued to ride 'topsides'.

Mines also became the nightmare of foot soldiers. Jungle paths and road verges were obvious places in which to lay mines and estimates of American ground soldier fatalities from them range between 16 and 30 per cent. In the latter half of 1968 57 per cent of all casualties in the US 1st Marine Division were attributed to mines and booby traps.[29]. To avoid mines, soldiers were encouraged to cut through thick jungle rather than risk using paths, as a wartime verse explained:

> 'Here's to our brave Corporal Pine.
> He was in such a rush,
> He couldn't cut through the bush.
> Cause of death: a well-placed mine'[30]

The increasing use of helicopters to transport troops to fighting areas prompted the first use of anti-helicopter mines. The Vietcong improvised the 'Cong Truong', a fragmentation mine initiated by the pressure of rotor blade down-draft on two tin plates. To blend in with the natural vegetation, the plates were leaf-shaped and painted green. The anti-helicopter mine was placed on likely landing zones and was capable of spraying shrapnel through an aircraft's fuselage.

To counter this threat, spectacular explosive countermeasures were developed. The first involved massive (up to 8,000lb) blast bombs capable of blowing a landing zone in thick jungle or destroying any mines and enemy soldiers in an existing one. In 1971 more efficient fuel–air explosives (FAE) were developed. FAEs were delivered by helicopter in a cluster bomb unit and on detonation caused a surface over-pressure of 22kg/sq. cm over a 182sq. m area.

While the Vietcong used mines to attack aircraft, the United States started to use aircraft to deliver mines, initially using a direct copy of the German SD 2. The Germans may have lacked confidence in the mine/bomblet concept, but by the 1960s it was appreciated that it had an advantage over single, large bombs in that a larger area could be attacked with a greater chance of engaging a dispersed enemy. Using hundreds of air-dropped frag-mentation devices in a single payload an area 400m long and 200m wide could be saturated with steel splinters, slicing all flesh in the vicinity and by fitting some bomblets with delay action fuzes the area remained hazardous for extended periods.

The Americans dropped thousands of bomblets, improving on the SD 2 (whose 'butterfly wings' frequently caught in trees) with more streamlined versions: BLU 2, BLU 3, BLU 24, BLU 26 and BLU 61.[31] A large percentage of these failed to explode and were collected by the Vietcong who used them as mines against their senders. Most famously, the BLU 2 was transformed into the fragmentation mine the B40 'apple mine' and is still encountered in Cambodia.

At this point mine warfare advanced a further and disturbing step. Not content with the instantaneous effect of fragmentation bomblets, it was appreciated that the same area could remain hazardous for extended periods (forever?) if mines were dropped in the same fashion. To achieve this an air-dropped mine system known as the BLU 43 was developed. This was nicknamed the 'Dragonstooth' on account of its angular 'W' shape. It was delivered in batches of forty containers each holding 120 of the small (20g) pressure-operated mines. (A close copy of the Dragon-stooth was made by the Soviets, known as the PFM-1; many were dropped on Afghanistan.)

Air-dropped mines had several distinct advantages over their ground-emplaced relations: they could be deployed quickly, they required little logistic support and they could be laid deep within enemy-held territory. Undoubtedly they caused casualties and disrupted some Vietcong movement, but any subsequent advance into the area by the Americans was equally hazardous. The location of air-dropped mines could not be marked and efficient communication was required to ensure that American forces avoided contaminated areas. Thus the use of these systems rendered land useless to friend and foe alike and, of course, to civilians – even after the war. With no self-neutralizing mechanism or easy clearance technique, these mines represented a modern version of the ancient, reviled practice of poisoning wells or ploughing salt into farmland.

In fact, air-dropped mines were not well suited for use against the Vietcong whose movements were frequently unknown and there are no reports of any tactical advantage gained through their use. However, the principle had been demonstrated and it was appreciated that, given the right circumstances, air-scatterable mines had a role to play.

Although there is no documentary evidence to indicate the Vietcong experience with American mines, it is clear that the Vietcong's remained a persistent and vexing problem for the Americans. The Vietcong took the mine out of its traditional role of enhancing defensive positions and used it to attack and to harass. As a consequence the Americans not only took many casualties, they were forced to allocate a significant portion of their manpower to mitigating the threat and had to invent a series of costly countermeasures that never proved entirely satisfactory. As the Second World War saw the mixed minefield firmly embedded into the defensive doctrine of conventional armies, so the Vietnam War established the mine as a major offensive weapon of guerrilla forces. Technology and manpower could be countered by simplicity and stealth.

The Yom Kippur War

On 6 October 1973 the fiercest of all the Arab–Israeli wars erupted while the Israelis celebrated the Yom Kippur holiday, leaving their frontiers defended by only a small number of reserve troops. Israel's borders were protected by minefields combined with anti-tank ditches, but they were rapidly penetrated by the Arab armies using flails and ploughs while massive firepower suppressed the defenders. The Israelis underestimated the Arabs' ability to mount a co-ordinated suprise offensive and overestimated the ability of minefields to stop attacks. The Israelis appreciated how devastating minefields could be, having encountered them in the war of 1956. At Alm Ageila half a company of Israeli half-tracks was destroyed by mines and the remainder were so constrained by them that they could not find cover from anti-tank weapons. Again, in the war of 1967 an Israeli offensive had foundered on Egyptian minefields at Um Katah. In 1973 the Arabs demonstrated that with well-planned countermeasures and sufficient firepower the story could be reversed.

Quick to respond to the surprise attack during Yom Kippur, the Israelis counterattacked brilliantly and rapidly reversed the advance of the Arab armies. In one engagement the Egyptian 25th Armoured Brigade was caught in the Sinai between an Israeli force and one of the original defensive minefields. The Egyptians lost eighty-six T-62 tanks and all its APCs, 'the minefield was used as an anvil for an armoured hammer'.[32]

The Yom Kippur War was carefully studied by defence analysts who always regarded Arab–Israeli wars as providing an approximation of the form of battle that could occur between Warsaw Pact and NATO forces in western Europe. The main themes were the suprise attack and the speed of battle. These alerted strategists to the requirements for sound intelligence, rapid communications and instant response to attack. The ease with which defences were breached did not necessarily indicate that minefields were futile. It was suggested that, had the troops on the border had sufficient anti-tank weapons, they might have slowed the Arabs considerably. The issue of the utility of mines in the war was debated, but several American studies indicated that the way ahead was to deliver scatterable mines in front of an attack before clearance assets could be deployed or behind a retreat in order to take advantage of the hammer-and-anvil tactic.[33]

Technical Developments

In the event of hostilities in western Europe, NATO forces planned to lay massive minefields across West Germany. In the absence of any other method it was planned to lay these by hand, a very time-consuming, labour-intensive process. A thousand-yards-long minefield containing 1,250 British Mark 7 anti-tank mines, weighing a total of 17 tonnes, would take a squadron of ninety sappers two and a half hours to lay. During the 1950s a number of methods of mechanical minelaying were introduced to speed up the process, starting with simple chutes attached to the rear of a vehicle from which mines could be surface laid. During the 1960s ploughs were introduced to open a furrow in the ground and replace soil over buried mines.

In 1972 the British Army briefly took the lead in mechanical mine-laying technology with the introduction of the L9A1 Barmine system. The concept was borrowed from the German *Riegelmine* 43, which, it will be recalled, was a barmine capable of being initiated by pressure upon any part of its length. The British appreciated the economy of this system, with a length of 1.2m, only half as many mines were required to achieve the same kill ratio in a minefield as with conventional, round mines. Furthermore, its shape lent itself to convenient packaging and, more importantly, to mechanical laying. A troop of thirty sappers could lay a thousand-yards minefield with 655 barmines, weighing 7.2 tonnes, in an hour.

Initially the Barmine was used in conjunction with the Canadian C3A1[34] 'Elsie' anti-personnel mine, which was issued in 1962. The C3A1 offered improvements over the Second World War mines in that it was made of plastic (although it did have a removable metal detection ring) and was very small – 51mm in diameter and 71mm long. For rapid laying, rather than having to be dug into the ground, it could be pushed in with a boot heel and then have its charge inserted. Furthermore, the explosive charge at 7.6g was probably the smallest in any mine. For military planners, laying the Elsie was still too slow and in 1976 the British brought the Ranger scatterable-mine system into service.

This was a vehicle-mounted system which could fire 1,296 plastic-cased, anti-personnel mines a hundred metres. Its main purpose was to cover an anti-tank minefield or create instant 'nuisance' minefields on demolition sites or roads. The combination of Barmine and Ranger offered great economies in manpower and logistic effort but the system was still too slow to be used in a surprise attack scenario and it did not take advantage of new electronic-fuse technology.

In 1974 the French army introduced the HPD anti-tank mine. Like the Barmine, it could be mechanically laid but it featured a Miznay-Shardin shaped charge capable of attacking the whole width of a tank. The significant difference from the US M21 was that it used a seismic- and magnetic-influence fuze rather than a tilt rod and was self-neutralizing after thirty-one days in the ground. As the mine acted against the entire width of a tank, rather than just on its tracks, half as many HPDs as Barmines[35] were required to cover the same area and its shaped-charge effect usually destroyed rather than immobilized a tank. Although a US handbook did warn that 'because an explosive force [using a Miznay-Shardin plate] is extremely concentrated, there is a possibility that the drive mechanism may escape damage. In this case, the tank may continue to move forward even though its crew had been killed.'[36]

As the Yom Kippur War demonstrated, the rapid pace of war could quickly make minefields redundant. Circumstances were envisaged whereby it might be advantageous to counterattack through a minefield. A breach could be ploughed or flailed through one's own minefields, but this would mean allocating additional resources and counterattacking in a vulnerable file formation. Far more useful would be the ability to neutralize one's own mines at predetermined periods. The Swedish Army was the first to exploit this concept with its FFV 028 mines. Each mine was blast-resistant, magnetic-influence fuzed, contained a shaped charge and could be laid by hand or mechanically. Most significantly, it had a self-neutralizing system which enabled it to be armed or disarmed at preset times of from 30 to 180 days. With its high metal content the mine could be easily located and its self-neutralizing mechanism allowed for its safe removal. It was in service with the Swedes by 1982 and the system was subsequently purchased (at a cost of around $500 per mine) by the German and the Dutch Army.

During the 1970s three Italian companies, Valsella, Technovar and Misar, started to manufacture and to market aggressively a range of mines utilizing state-of-the-art fuze mechanisms and modern plastics. The Italians assimilated the lessons of Vietnam and Yom Kippur and realized that in many circumstances even mechanically-laid minefields did not offer sufficient economies of manpower or operational flexibility. A solution, as the United States had indicated, was the helicopter-delivered, scatterable system. This was first offered by Misar in 1978 with the basic module containing 2,496 anti-personnel mines, 160 anti-tank mines or a combination of both. The anti-personnel mine was the virtually non-detectable SB 33, which featured an anti-shock device that made it insensitive to explosive clearance. Optional extras included a choice of colour, a special paint that made it undetectable to infra-red equipment and an anti-handling device. The anti-tank mine was the SB 81, containing all the features of the SB 33 but with an additional option of self-neutralization. The other Italian companies produced similar concepts and sold around forty different types of mine during the 1970s and the 1980s. Many of these mines, it should be noted, were beautifully formed from resilient plastic with bold ribs and textured pressure plates; they appeared to have been sculpted rather than manufactured and they offered a stylish alternative to the fashion-conscious mine layer. The Italian helicopter-delivered systems were a significant improvement on mechanically-laid minefields; but, due to their vulnerability to ground fire, they could be used only in areas held by friendly forces.

Following Vietnam, the Americans had been busy testing a variety of scatterable systems delivered by ground launcher, helicopter, supersonic aircraft and artillery. The aim was to produce a 'family of scatterable mines' or FASCAM, capable of meeting the demands of modern, fast-paced war. Apart from rapid deployment, all the FASCAM mines featured self-destruct systems, common parts and maximum lethality. The concept was designed to overcome unfavourable force ratios, counter surprise attacks and extract maximum attrition from an enemy at ranges where direct-fire weapons were ineffective. Early designs incorporating the new concept included the supersonic-aircraft-delivered BLU 42 and 54 fragmenting, anti-personnel mine system (the replacement for the Dragonstooth), and the helicopter-delivered M56 pressure-activated, anti-tank mine system, incorporating an anti-disturbance fuse. While vulnerable, helicopter-delivered systems remained useful for closing gaps in minefields or rapidly creating nuisance minefields.

By the late 1970s earlier designs were improved to enable reliable delivery by supersonic aircraft, which were less vulnerable than helicopters and provided an interdiction capability behind enemy lines. In 1981 the Gator system, incorporating the BLU 91/B anti-tank mine and the BLU 92/B anti-personnel mine, was brought into service. The BLU 91/B featured a Miznay-Shardin plate combined with a magnetic-influence fuse. The BLU 92/B launched a series of tripwires after landing and formed lethal fragments when disturbed. A single aircraft could deliver 564 mines at once, covering an area 300m by 200m. The Gator system was capable of isolating objectives, countering artillery fire, denying terrain, disrupting support activities and inflicting personnel and equipment losses. 'With its speed and responsiveness it is one of the most influential systems on the battlefield', stated a US Army handbook, 'But the high cost required for such a sophisticated system may limit the availability of munitions.'[37] The humble mine had been transformed into a highly effective and versatile weapon system – for those who could afford it.

Early additions to the FASCAM were the area-denial artillery munitions (ADAM) and the remote anti-armour mine system (RAAMS). Delivered by a 155mm howitzer to a range of over 17km, much less than their jet-aircraft-delivered cousins, but also less vulnerable, cheaper and faster to respond. Each ADAM artillery round contained thirty-six bounding fragmentation mines initiated by trip wire. The RAAMS round contained nine magnetic-influenced mines, each with a shaped charge. Artillery-delivered mines could be used for a wide range of tasks, including supplementing protective fire and restricting enemy mobility.

While mine laying had been elevated from the earth-bound sapper to the sky-streaking pilot, a significant role remained for the former. The laying of large tactical minefields in areas controlled by friendly forces was still best achieved from the ground as this ensured accuracy, thoroughness, economy and the ability to mark the danger area physically. To speed up the tedious laying process the M128 ground-emplaced, mine-scattering system (GEMSS) was developed. This was capable of throwing 800 mines every fifteen minutes up to 90m and one of five minefield density selections was available ranging from 0.001 to 0.250 mines/sq. m. The system employed the M75 anti-tank and the M74 anti-personnel mine (similar to the RAAMS and the BLU 92 Gator mine). GEMSS was clearly a scatterable system and ran contrary to the then conventional philosophy that tactical minefields should incorporate buried mines. However, given the relatively small size of the mines (about 12cm diameter), together with the limited visibility and intense activity on the battlefield, it was considered that the visual location of mines by the enemy did not pose a significant limitation to their effectiveness.

By the 1980s mines had assimilated all aspects of modern technology and become an integral part of fast-paced manoeuvre warfare. Air- and artillery-delivered mines would have undoubtedly played a major role in stopping Arab forces during the Yom Kippur War. It is often said that the military always plan for the previous war and this example proves the point.

War in Rhodesia

While Western armies were concentrating their focus as regards mine warfare on the countering of surprise attacks by massed armoured formations, other conflicts had been developing in a different direction. Vietnam had demonstrated the problems caused by mines in guerrilla warfare and the lesson had been repeated in nationalist struggles against the colonial masters in Aden, Cyprus, Mozambique and Angola. By the early 1970s Rhodesia, which had unilaterally declared independence in 1965 against hostile world opinion, was struggling against nationalist guerrillas employing offensive mining tactics. Surrounded by hostile states and experiencing an international embargo, Rhodesians were forced to provide a solution to a problem which had vexed the Americans, the British and the Portuguese. Although very much an intra-state conflict, the Rhodesian experience is related here because of the innovative manner in which the white Rhodesians attempted to counter the threat.

The first mine attacks in Rhodesia came in 1972 and continued with increasing frequency until the end of the war in 1980. In that time there were 2,405 recorded instances of anti-tank mines being detonated by a variety of vehicles, killing 632 and injuring 4,410 people. The white Rhodesians were as vulnerable to mine attacks as the Americans had been in Vietnam. The vast expanse of the African bush, dissected by only a few, mostly dirt roads, was ideal terrain for offensive mining. A man with a single TM46 mine could be as effective as a supersonic aircraft and a payload of sophisticated scatterable mines. With only unarmoured wheeled vehicles for transport, the effects of detonating an anti-tank mine were spectacular for the guerrilla but lethal for the occupants.

Tough, determined and with no line of retreat, the Rhodesians faced the problem with great ingenuity. They concentrated their efforts first on protecting the occupants of vehicles from the effects of a mine blast. This had been attempted by both the Americans and the British in the past. General Patton attended one demonstration in Tunisia in 1943 where a goat was tethered inside a prototype blast resistant vehicle while a *Tellermine* was detonated underneath it. The official report noted that 'the goat died bravely'[38] but no significant developments had been made in this difficult area. In Rhodesia the ubiquitous Landrover was fitted with metal plates to deflect blast, rubber matting to absorb it and roll bars to prevent crush injuries if the vehicle turned over. This reduced the rate of occupant fatalities from 22 to 7.5 per cent.[39] It was a big improvement but 47 per cent of vehicle occupants were still wounded in mine blasts and the vehicle was normally destroyed. Filling the tyres with water to help in deflecting pressure waves improved the situation slightly, but it was clear that more radical modifications were required.

The major breakthrough came with the adoption of a 'V' shaped vehicle hull, strong enough to deflect a blast and leave the occupants unscathed if they were securely strapped in. The pioneering work in this field was carried out in South Africa and about 150 models of the Hyena – the first mine-protected truck –

were purchased by the Rhodesians. The improvement over the mine-protected Landrover was striking: of 140 Hyenas blown up only two people were killed out of a total of 578 occupants – a fatality rate of 0.3 per cent. However, the injury rate at 21 per cent remained high and the vehicle engine, again, was normally destroyed by the blast.

The next stage in development was the introduction of the monocoque principle, adapted by Ernest Konshel in a four-seater vehicle known as the Leopard. The Leopard's engine and crew compartment were contained within a single hull with the axles mounted externally. A mine could destroy an axle but left the rest of the vehicle relatively unscathed and the damage could be repaired quickly and cheaply. The design proved very successful and was applied to other small vehicles, including the Cougar, the Ojay and the Kudu and trucks such as the Puma and the Crocodile. Mine-protected vehicles of this type returned similar fatality and injury rates to the Hyena: 0.6 and 18.5 per cent, respectively. But of considerable significance to a country with no external support, mined vehicles could rapidly be made serviceable without an extensive logistical effort. The monocoque was undoubtedly a success and enabled the Rhodesians to continue the war by preserving men and resources and providing a significant level of confidence to soldiers on operations.

Although mine-protected vehicles greatly limited the damage caused by mines, the preferable solution was to locate the mines before they caused any damage. Clearing roads with conventional tactics was, of course, slow and demanded a huge number of men. Attempts were made to cover roads with dye so that any movement on or across them was immediately obvious. This technique, though cheaper than using black top, required frequent reapplications and returned only marginal benefits. The eventual solution was a monocoque fitted with wide, racing-car tyres which spread the weight of the vehicle sufficiently so that it would not detonate a mine. A simple but highly effective modification, the new vehicle was named the Pookie. Its potential was immediately realized and mine detectors were fitted to the vehicle, enabling it to locate the guerrillas' most common mine, the metal-cased TM 46, without detonating it. Previous schemes of this sort had foundered because they were applied in environments with considerable metal contamination against mines with a very small metal content. In Rhodesia the detectors could be calibrated to give an alarm only on large metal objects and the Pookie could travel quickly because to stop in time to avoid driving over a mine was not a problem. In four years of operational service Pookie detection teams located 550 mines.

The inevitable response of the guerrillas was to switch to non-metallic mines which effectively thwarted the Pookie's ability to detect them. Command-detonated mines were also used to stop the Pookie and, while these usually left the operator unscathed, the Pookie's thin armour made it vulnerable to subsequent attack by large-calibre small arms or an RPG7. In response to the non-metallic mine the Rhodesians invented a detector to locate these but little is known of its efficiency.

The Americans had discovered in Vietnam that the best way of reducing attacks was to mount aggressive patrols. The Rhodesians recognized this but with only limited manpower it was a difficult policy to sustain. It was therefore decided to isolate guerrilla support from neighbouring countries by laying minefields along the border. Due to the international embargo, mines were made in small workshops throughout the country, including copies of the Soviet PMD 6 and the British No.6. One of the home-made mines, an original design known as the Ploughshare, was considered good enough to market internationally after the war. The border minefields were only partly complete by the end of the war and were of limited success. There was insufficient manpower to cover them effectively and the guerrillas were able to breach them repeatedly. Furthermore, carcasses in the minefield indicated that animals had become mine victims.

In the Rhodesian war offensive mining was never countered completely but it was certainly tamed to a greater extent than in other, similar conflicts. Through the use of mine-protected vehicles, the white security forces were able to project their strength into the countryside, and, although they still incurred casualties, mines did not induce the same level of caution as was experienced by the Americans in Vietnam. The Rhodesians and the South Africans had become world leaders in mine-protected vehicles, but few other armies required the technology. Lightly-armoured wheeled vehicles did not feature in NATO or Warsaw Pact battle plans and monocoque construction could not be easily applied to tracks. NATO was equipped to fight a modern, general war not a protracted guerrilla campaign. The Rhodesian war stands alone as an illuminating example of how to contain offensive mining, but at the time the lesson appeared to have little relevance to anyone else. However, in recent years peace-keeping forces have started to purchase mine-protected vehicles for operations in Angola, Cambodia and Bosnia where mined roads represent a considerable hazard.

The Gulf War

On 2 August 1990 Iraqi forces swarmed over the border into neighbouring Kuwait, precipitating international military action to liberate the occupied country. Expelling the Iraqis appeared to be a daunting task: the country had a large army and six months in which to prepare its defences. With no natural barriers along the southern border of Kuwait, the Iraqis followed the example of the armies in the North African desert in World War Two and laid extensive minefields. They used a mixture of old and relatively modern mines. Anti-tank mines included metal-cased TM46s and TM62s, minimum-metal PT Mi Ba III and P2 Mk 3 and T72s and the Italian minimum-metal, blast-resistant mines the VS1.6 and the VS2.2. The latter in particular caused some concern as it was uncertain whether it contained anti-disturbance or magnetic-influence options. Anti-personnel mines included the Soviet PMN, the Chinese Type 72A and the Type 72B version with anti-handling device, the Italian SB33, VS 50 and TS50 (all blast-resistant) and the Italian bounding fragmentation mines the V69 and the P40.

Probably fewer than two million mines were laid,[40] most of them in well-organized fields and often fenced. The format was entirely conventional and they contained no surprises. The minefields were covered with fire and the overall defence was developed in considerable depth, although the minefields themselves were probably not sufficiently wide. The layout was reminiscent of the German pattern at El Alamein. As the Allies faced those minefields with deep concern, so did the Coalition forces who faced the Iraqi minefields in Kuwait.

Many advances had been made in mine laying but clearance had not received similar attention. The British had phased out flails in 1965 in favour of the Giant Viper rocket-propelled explosive hose. (In the same year the bounding fragmentation mines was also phased out as the British considered that it had 'little value in general war'.) The Giant Viper could clear a path 185m long and 7.5m wide; but while it was one of the most spectacular battlefield systems in existence it was of limited use against blast-resistant mines. In the mid-1980s the British had again experimented with flails and in the absence of adequate mine countermeasures in the Gulf, about twenty Aardvark flail half-tracks were rapidly brought into service. There were insufficient mine ploughs for the British armoured force and more of these too had to be purchased rapidly and adapted to fit a variety of vehicles. To counter the possible threat of magnetic-influence-fused mines, the MIMIC (magnetic-influence mine-clearance device) was acquired and fitted to engineer tanks.[41] The British discovered that they had also been complacent about manual mine clearance. In 1990 the British Army was still using the 4C detector, closely related to the original Polish model and last updated in 1968. It was woefully inadequate for locating minimum-metal mines and it was not until after the war that modern AN/19 Schiebel detectors were made available.

American countermeasures were little better. They had three different types of explosive hose: the APOBS (anti-personnel obstacle-breaching system) capable of clearing a lane 45m long and 0.6m wide through anti-personnel mines; the M58 MICLIC (mine-clearing line charge), similar to but smaller than the Giant Viper, it could clear a lane 100m long and 6m wide; and the M154 triple shot line charge, capable of clearing a 300m by 8m lane. Like their British cousin, they were not effective against blast-resistant or double-impulse mines. One hundred and eighteen mine ploughs were issued to American units in the Gulf and these were mounted on M1 and M60 tanks and M728 combat engineer vehicles. Mine rollers were tested in the desert but were not used in combat because they were slow, cumbersome and their excessive weight resulted in their getting stuck in soft sand.[42]

Concern about mines led to a number of field improvisations. Faced with the threat of seismic- and magnetic-influence-fuzed mines without a countermeasure, the Americans built VEMASID (vehicle magnetic signature duplicator) in the field. This was fabricated from 1,450ft of wire coiled on a 5ft by 4ft tray with power drawn from a slave receptacle and mounted between the mine ploughs of a tank. Other improvisations included the fashioning of non-metallic mine probes from tent pegs, the use of commercial leaf blowers to uncover mines in sand, and crossbow-launched grapnels fired into minefields to pull tripwires.[43]

Before the land battle the Coalition forces waged an extremely effective air campaign. This immediately gained air supremacy, destroyed a large amount of equipment and demoralized the defenders to such an extent that they were unable to resist the Coalition juggernaut when it finally rolled across the border. The air campaign included efforts in support of the breaching operation: B52s dropped Mk 117 (750lb) and Mk 82 (500lb) bombs and the US Marine Corps (USMC) dropped 254 550lb FAE bombs and a number of 15,000lb bombs in an attempt to detonate mines, but these efforts had 'little impact on minefields'.[44]

After a six-weeks' air campaign the Coalition forces advanced into Kuwait but encountered few Iraqis prepared to fight. The much feared minefields were breached rapidly, mostly by American forces who used a variety of techniques. The Marine Corps used forty-nine APOBSs and fifty-five M-154s, but only about half of the latter were successfully deployed and neither equipment was effective (quite predictably) against blast-resistant mines. Combat engineer vehicles were used to doze aside the remaining mines.[45] Despite these efforts, the USMC 6 Division lost eleven vehicles, including seven tanks, and fourteen men were wounded.[46] The US Army depended heavily from the start on the use of full-width mine ploughs, which proved exceptionally effective in the soft sand and created easily visible lanes for follow-on forces.

That the Iraqi minefields had barely delayed the Coalition forces in their attack was more a testament to Coalition air and ground firepower than the effectiveness of mine countermeasures. The mine clearance methods were little more sophisticated than they had been in 1945. An American observer commented, 'the

US Army entered a state of countermine comatose [*sic*]. It was a coma so deep and widespread among the branches, that to this day the US Army has not fielded a single new countermine system.'[47]

Given that brute strength could neutralize the barrier minefield, does it still have a role to play in defence? Arguably yes, while 'the stronger force always prevails', mines, even in Kuwait, added to the strain of war – additional fear was created, movement was inhibited, and extra *matériel*, training and co-ordination were required. Although ultimately peripheral to the Gulf War, barrier minefields were the only means of enhancing defence available to the Iraqis. Like the Israelis in the Yom Kippur War, the Iraqis discovered that barrier minefields were effective only to the extent that they were actively defended.

During the Gulf War FASCAM was used for the first time. A total of 1,314 Gator units were dropped on Iraqi positions to prevent movement and behind Iraqi positions to prevent withdrawal or reinforcement: a classic example of the armoured (and airborne) hammer trapping an enemy against the anvil of mines. The ADAM and the RAAMS artillery-delivered system were also deployed to the Gulf, but it is uncertain whether they too were fired. At short notice, to provide flank protection during the advance, the British acquired the German Skorpian scatterable-mine system. Capable of creating an anti-tank mine barrier with 600 mines over an area 1,500m long and 50m wide in five minutes – considerably more versatile than the ageing Ranger – it was apparently not used during the war. The British did, however, use the JP233 runway-denial system on Iraqi airfields. This contained a mixture of shaped-charge bombs to shatter a runway and mines with timed fuses and anti-disturbance devices to prevent rapid runway repair. A total of 106 were dropped. One alarming feature of scatterable systems in general and their self-destruct systems in particular was their failure rate. The presence of Gator mines across the Kuwaiti desert was highly apparent after the war and an estimated 10 per cent of all these mines did not self-destruct – fifty-six mines from each of the hundreds of units dropped.

Similar scatterable systems would doubtless have been useful to the Iraqis. The sudden appearance of a scatterable minefield would have slowed the momentum of the Coalition advance and the Americans concluded that they would have had no way of countering such mines 'if these had been encountered away from a deliberate breach site':[48] a significant conclusion reinforcing the fact that the development of countermeasures lagged far behind that of delivery systems and the high-tech generation of mines.

The land battle lasted seventy-two hours, after which mines started to take their toll. Curious soldiers and civilians exploring and trophy hunting around abandoned Iraqi positions wandered unwittingly into minefields, some of which had become indistinct from the rest of the desert as sand drifted over fences and warning signs. Within six months of the end of the war 70 Coalition soldiers had been killed and a further 360 injured on mines and unexploded ordnance; this may be compared with the fewer than 150 Coalition soldiers killed during the actual conflict. By 1993 around 1,700 civilians had also been killed by mines and unexploded ordnance along with an unknown number of sheep, camels and goats.[49]

Uniquely, the minefields and unexploded ordnance in Kuwait was cleared almost exclusively by foreign troops or commercial contractors paid for by the Kuwait government. Commercial contractors from the USA, the United Kingdom and France, along with troops from Egypt, Pakistan, Turkey and Bangladesh, were involved in the clearance operation which cost the Kuwaiti government an estimated $7–800 million. The mine clearance, as it had been after the Second World War, was conducted largely with metal detectors and probes. The techniques for breaching the minefields were unsuitable for clearing entire fields. Explosive hoses were ineffective on blast-proof mines and ploughs simply pushed mines aside, leaving them buried at unpredictable angles and causing further difficulties for mine clearers. The British company Royal Ordnance did attempt to use flails but the combination of resilient, plastic-cased mines and soft sand resulted in the mines being driven deeper into the sand or hurled away from the machine. The French demonstrated a thorough but labour-intensive approach in using entrenching tools in a side-sweeping motion to scrape lanes through minefields. Sand was pulled behind the mine clearer and mines struck on their sides did not detonate. The method was much faster than probing and often much more reliable than a metal detector, especially when working with minimum-metal mines. In the age of the Stealth bomber it seemed ironic, if not tragic, that such primitive methods were still necessary.

Conclusions

In the five decades since the end of the Second World War the mine gained increasing importance on the battlefield. Its effect was never decisive, but always influential, subtle, but never insignificant. The most notable recent development has been the ability to lay minefields as rapidly as the tactical situation changed without great logistic effort. This not only expanded the mine's traditional defensive role but also provided an interdiction capability. Paradoxically, while a technologically-advanced army could deliver mines deep within enemy territory, guerrilla armies were capable of paralysing strong conventional forces by the cunning use of mines. Even the simplest of mines defied rapid detection and removal. The contrast between the sophistication of modern mines and the primitive counter-mine methods is quite striking. Given the range of tactical situations, terrain and types of force that used them, mines have undoubtedly been one of the most flexible weapon systems of the late twentieth century.

References and Notes

1. Donovan and Moat, p. 5.
2. Ibid.
3. Engineer Agency for Resource Inventories, Vol.5, Appendix cc.
4. Maj. R.I. Crawford, quoted in Westover, pp. 24–5.
5. Capt G.R. Spreng, quoted in Westover, p. 42.
6. Lt S.D. Starobin, quoted in Westover, p. 23.
7. Robert J. O'Neil, *Australia in the Korean War, 1950–53* (Australian Government Publishing Service, 1985), pp. 253–4.
8. Engineer Agency for Resource Inventories, Vol.5, p.B1.
9. Quoted in Sloan, p. 2.
10. Maj. R.I. Crawford, quoted in Westover, p. 25.
11. Engineer Agency for Resource Inventories, Vol.5, p. A3.
12. Maj. D.F. Crawford, quoted in Westover, p. 27.
13. A pressure-operated fragmenting mine with a square-sided, cast-iron body.

14. Maj. D.F. Campbell Crawford, quoted in Westover, p. 30.
15. Copies of the German *Holzmine* 42 and *Schu* mine, respectively.
16. Raschen, p. 96.
17. Ibid, p. 97.
18. Department of the Army (1966), p. 2–1.
19. Hay, p. 131.
20. Frost, p. 97.
21. Ibid., p. 95.
22. Quoted in ibid., p. 95.
23. Starry, p. 79.
24. Hay, p. 131.
25. Starry, p. 82.
26. R. Lubow, in Westing, pp. 73–4.
27. Engineer Agency for Resource Inventories, Vol.9, p. 57.
28. Westing, p. 81.
29. US Department of State (1994), p. 7.
30. Quoted in Engineer Agency for Resource Inventories, Vol.9, p.c273.
31. The Vietnamese named bomblets after the fruit they resembled: BLU 2 – apple; BLU 3 – pineapple; BLU 24 – orange; BLU 26 – guava. In the US military coding BLU indicates Bombs and Mines Unit.
32. Sloan, pp. 6–7.
33. Cordesman and Wagner, Vol.1, p. 71.
34. To remember foreign nomenclatures, ordnance technicians claim that 'C' is for Canadian, 'M' is for 'Merican and 'L' is for Limey.
35. A bolt-on fuze with a full-width attack capability was manufactured by Marconi in the late 1970s for use with the Barmine.
36. Department of the Army, FM 20–32, pp. 71–2.
37. Ibid., p. 95.
38. Mayo, p. 155.
39. Stiff; this is a valuable source of statistics and provides an insight into the development of Southern African mine-protected vehicles.
40. Estimates range between 0.5 million (Cordesman) and 5–7 million (Vietnam Veterans of America).
41. Beaton, *Royal Engineers Journal*, Vol.105, No.3, December 1991, p. 269.
42. Cordesman and Wagner, Vol.4, pp. 740–1.
43. Schneck, pp. 2–7.
44. Cordesman and Wagner, Vol.4, p. 519.
45. Ibid, p. 606.
46. Atkinson, p. 375.
47. Sickler, p. 11.
48. Cordesman and Wagner, Vol.4, p. 741.
49. Donovan, p. 222.

Chapter 7

Intra-state Conflicts and Humanitarian Issues

Proliferation

During the 1970s and the 1980s a number of intra-state conflicts raged in parts of the developing world. The typical scenario was a guerrilla group opposing a Soviet-backed state government in a low-technology, low-intensity but protracted war. Countries such as Cambodia, Afghanistan, Mozambique, Angola and Somalia were host to such conflicts. Details of the wars were often sketchy, but the steady flow of refugees into neighbouring countries was an indication of the level of suffering endured. Among the many miseries related by refugees it became clear that landmines were a significant cause of concern. The modern intra-state conflict in the developing world promoted a different style of mine warfare from that of conventional war, as Soviet military doctrine reacted to guerrilla warfare.

Soviet defensive philosophy was profoundly shaped by the German invasion of the Soviet Union in 1941. Mines played a significant role in halting the Germans and henceforth they were considered indispensable for defence. By the mid-1970s Warsaw Pact forces had over fifty different types of mine in their inventories. Most were fairly simple devices, cheap to manufacture and easy to use, even by soldiers with limited training.[1] In addition to the creation of barrier minefields in front of an enemy, it was standard practice for Soviet forces to protect the perimeters of airfields, barracks, bridges and other potential targets with a belt of anti-personnel mines – a practice they exported to developing countries. The Chinese also adopted the Soviet mass mine-laying doctrine, quaintly described in a manual dating from about 1980:

'In the aggressive war, the imperialists and all their running dogs will surely use numerous technical equipment such as tanks, armoured cars, etc. to launch an offensive by a mobile surprise attack at high speed. Therefore . . . the employment of vast numbers of mines will remain to be one of the important means of struggling against the enemy.'

When exporting military technology, only part of the Soviet weapons arsenal was appropriate to the tactical situation and the environment of the developing world. There was a limited requirement for armour, artillery, jet aircraft or ballistic missiles as neither the terrain nor the anticipated enemy threat lent themselves to these weapons. Furthermore the developing world had insufficient infrastructure, technicians, finance or organization to support high-technology military imports. Combat in the developing world was best suited to foot soldiers using light weapons such as the AK 47 assault rifle, the RPG 7 shoulder-launched, anti-tank rocket-propelled grenade, the mortar and the landmine. After all, a similarly equipped Vietcong had brought the United States to its knees in Vietnam.

Guerrilla warfare generally consists of a series of raids by small groups of lightly-armed irregulars who live in remote areas or among sympathetic villagers. Because of their limited resources they attack easy, often civilian targets, forcing governments to deploy large numbers of troops and act in an authoritarian manner towards the general populace who cannot be distinguished from the civilian-clothed guerrillas. To protect settlements from guerrilla attack, many were ringed with anti-personnel mines. Generally these were laid by soldiers with little training or education and consequently few minefields were recorded or marked.[2] Furthermore, government forces rarely saw any advantage in marking mines as these were the very weapons on which they relied, not just to deter their enemies but to kill them. As the conflicts progressed, government troops were rotated and new units laid more mines and the locations of older fields were forgotten. Around the town of Poipet on the Cambodia/Thai border three minefields were laid direct one on top of another by different military units over a period of ten years.[3] Retaining the population in rural settlements became a key government objective, as the depopulation of the countryside would result in the loss of agricultural production, an additional refugee burden and the abandonment of the land to the guerrillas.

Protective mine rings would certainly have inhibited a number of attacks and promoted a high degree of caution among guerrillas. Most guerrilla armies had few, if any, mine detectors and their surprise attacks could be made only following covert breaching operations involving the use of prodders. To further deter attacks, government troops laid mines across likely approach routes to settlements in an attempt to kill guerrillas before they reached their objective.

The protection of settlements tended to displace guerrilla activity to more vulnerable targets, such as roads where ambushes could be mounted. Roads are by nature difficult to defend and much manpower is required to guard them effectively. Placing mines at likely ambush points is economical, and, as the British discovered when using mines to protect railways in the Boer War, once the enemy start to initiate the mines, the frequency of attack drops dramatically.

Protracted guerrilla campaigns thus precipitated the widespread use by government troops of unmarked mines around settlements, infrastructure, jungle paths and road verges. In other words, mines were laid in all the areas close to human habitation.

The guerrilla forces used mines both offensively and defensively. If they lacked the strength to attack and hold a settlement, a handful of mines on the roads leading to it were sufficient to ensure that after the first vehicle hit a mine the road was never used again. As only a small percentage of the roads in the developing world were sealed and government forces lacked the resources to clear roads daily, this tactic effectively isolated towns and even entire regions. In Mozambique less than a quarter of the road system was sealed and of the unsealed portion 37 per cent was unused in 1994 due to the threat of mines.[4] Footpaths leading from government-held areas were also seeded with anti-personnel mines, thus making aggressive patrolling by government troops hazardous or even inhibiting it altogether. Additionally, approaches to guerrilla bases were mined to prevent penetration and to act as 'silent sentries'.

Pitched battles between guerrilla and government forces were infrequent and conflicts centred around the use of mines. The widespread nature of their use indicates that they were effective for both sides. Having originally been designed to enhance defensive positions, mines rapidly became the main weapon of war. The firefights in conflicts in the developing world were not fought by guns but by mines and both sides 'found themselves engaged in self destructive dependency'.[5] Given the nature of the conflict, mines were the only realistic means of defence.

The mines became a significant problem after the war because little or no effort was made to clear them and few if any records of them existed. Most mines were laid in close proximity to areas frequented by civilians and the victims of mines were often the very people whom they were supposed to protect. Returning refugees generally had no knowledge of mined areas and were especially prone to treading on them. People who remained in their homes during a conflict often had a good idea where mines were laid and were thus able to avoid them. However, while avoidance was possible, many had difficulty in evaluating the risk. A Red Cross study in north-west Cambodia in 1991/92 indicated that 73 per cent of mine victims knew that they had entered a mined area but still decided to take the risk.

That mines were not cleared by government forces at the end of conflict was the result of several factors. In general, many of the conflicts did not simply end, the security situation remained tense even after the official ceasefire and there was a general reluctance to dismantle defences. The end of many conflicts also coincided with the end of the Cold War and the withdrawal of Soviet assistance. Had the Soviets remained in the developing world they may well have organized mine clearance as they had in their own country at the end of the Second World War. Indeed, the Soviets had assisted in the clearance of Algeria in 1962 following the country's gaining of independence and the end of the conflict with France. With no outside assistance and exhausted by years of war, the governments of the developing world had no expertise or resources to clear mines. Furthermore, they did not immediately recognize uncleared mines as a significant problem until it was brought to their attention by international agencies. In Mozambique between 1980 and 1993 mine accidents caused only 3 per cent of accidental deaths, compared with suicide which accounted for 5 per cent and the major cause – road accidents – at 35 per cent.[6] While people in the developing world were twelve times more likely to die in a road accident than a mine accident, they were thirty times more likely to die of malaria, dysentery, anaemia or tuberculosis. Thus, as a public health issue, mine casualties were not considered especially significant.

Once international agencies started to get involved with the problem there was little incentive for the governments of developing countries to divert their limited resources to mine clearance. After the Vietnam War the government organized systematic clearance[7] itself and, although mine incidents are still reported, it appears to have largely contained the problem; however, in 1994 in Quang Tri Province sixteen people were killed and fifteen were injured by mines or unexploded ordnance. No other developing-world governments have had the resources, the ability or the will to clear mines. As many of the developing world conflicts pitched Western-backed guerrillas against Soviet-backed governments, it was hardly surprising that few countries had any qualms about waiting for Western aid agencies to act.

The misery and suffering caused by mines in the developing countries caught the imagination of the media and the Western world. Since the early 1990s the image of innocent and unsuspecting civilians mutilated by forgotten mines has haunted television screens around the world and many graphic accounts of the effects of landmines on civilian populations have been published.[8] Mines affect almost every aspect of life in countries emerging from conflict: they reduce agricultural production, prevent refugee return, hinder reconstruction, make roads impassable, cause large numbers of casualties and perpetuate the fear and anxiety caused by war.

The contrast between reactions to redundant minefields following the Second World War and those of the intra-state conflicts of the developing world was striking. In 1945 Europe quickly and energetically set about clearing the debris of war, without an excess of indignation. But the world five decades later was a very different, perhaps more humane place. Viewed from the comfort of a secure and wealthy Western world the suffering caused by mines in Africa, Asia and Central America prompted an irresistible, compassionate urge.

The Western Response

In response to what was perceived as a humanitarian crisis, Western-sponsored efforts were launched to mitigate the effects of mines. Initially this took the form of medical assistance to victims and was undertaken largely by the International Committee of the Red Cross (ICRC) which alerted the world to the problem of mines. It claimed that 'Mines may be described as fighters that never miss, strike blindly, do not carry weapons openly and go on killing long after hostilities have ended. In short, mines are the greatest violators of international humanitarian law, practising blind terrorism.'[9] In addition to medical assistance, the ICRC, followed by other groups such as Handicap International, organized prosthetic workshops to provide artificial limbs and rehabilitation to mine victims. Returning refugees were identified as one of the groups most likely to tread on mines and consequently mine-awareness campaigns were launched in refugee camps in an effort to educate people about the risks they ran.

While medical assistance and mine awareness were important elements in assisting mine-infested countries, the most crucial long-term objective was to remove the mines themselves. The first effort in this direction was the UN-sponsored *Operation Salam* in Pakistan between 1987 and 1989 which brought together foreign military engineers to train Afghan volunteers in mine clearance. After training over 13,000 Afghans it was concluded that the approach was unsuccessful because the trainees lacked the equipment and organization to clear mines once they had returned home.

In 1989 the UN Mine Clearance Program in Afghanistan changed its focus and started to co-ordinate mine clearance by relying on Afghan non-governmental organizations to conduct the work. By 1994 they had 2,800 personnel and an annual budget of around $25 million. In the same year the first charity of its kind, The HALO Trust, established a programme in northern Afghanistan which pioneered the format for humanitarian mine clearance which was duplicated elsewhere.

Inevitably, when embarking on clearance initiatives in Afghanistan the question arose as to how many mines had been laid. The short answer was that no one had any idea, consequently there was groundless speculation about numbers. Initial guesses were that 35 million had been laid but this later was rationalized to 10 million after Paul Jefferson, a British engineer working for the HALO Trust in Afghanistan, pointed out that 35 million was a great exaggeration. Even the more modest estimate of 10 million suggested that the Soviets had laid 3,000 mines per day, every day of the nine-year occupation, which, given the mountainous nature of the terrain and the style of the conflict, was unrealistically high. The decision to adopt the conveniently round figure of 10 million mines as the official estimate had far-reaching consequences.

When mine-clearance initiatives began in other countries estimates of the numbers of mines were measured against the benchmark of Afghanistan. It was felt that Cambodia was not as heavily mined as Afghanistan and a figure of 7 million was produced. Similarly, Mozambique was considered to be not nearly as heavily mined as Cambodia and a figure of 2 million mines was adopted. In fact it was soon appreciated that Mozambique probably had fewer than 300,000 mines; however, the United Nations continued to state the figure of 2 million officially in order to mobilize donor funding for the clearance programme – generally from organizations such as foreign ministries, the European Union and large charitable foundations.

The inflation of figures made clearance programmes look ineffective and grossly exaggerated the problem. In Afghanistan, where around 10,000 mines were being lifted annually, it was assumed and widely publicized that clearing 10 million mines would take a thousand years and donors shied away from adequately funding clearance because they viewed it as an open-ended commitment.

In fact, mine clearance agencies work in the much more reliable currency of square area. It takes about as long to clear a square kilometre of 100 mines as it does to clear the same area of 1,000. The disposing of individual mines can be achieved rapidly, but to search every square centimetre of land takes time. Surveys of Afghanistan during the early 1990s indicated that 466sq. km of land required clearance,[10] and the combined efforts of all agencies could clear around 25sq. km per year. This provides a much more accurate duration of less than twenty years to clear mines from the country; the increasing of staffing levels would obviously further reduce this time. In Cambodia the situation was similar: in 1994 the Cambodian Mine Action Centre claimed that 'It is expected that in 5–8 years the mine problem will be controlled and Cambodians can carry out their daily functions free from the threat of mines. Demining will continue at a reduced scale for probably 20 more years'.[11] However, the more reasonable estimates by specialists on the ground were ignored by the press and anti-mine campaigners. Any magnification of the figures could be justified in pursuit of a worthy cause.[12]

Caught between the desire to do something about the problem of mines and the need for long-term financial prudence, donors diverted modest amounts of cash towards mine clearance. This slowly increased as public awareness of the issue grew and from 1990 onwards a handful of mine-clearance charities (all non-government organizations) were formed, including the Mine Advisory Group (MAG), the Norwegian People's Aid (NPA), Kap Anamur and Menschen Gegen Minen (MGM). They established commendable grass-roots initiatives in many of the mine-affected countries. The United Nations instituted additional mine-clearance programmes in Cambodia, Mozambique, Angola and Bosnia.

With arms markets shrinking and armies shedding manpower as a result of the collapse of the Soviet Union, armaments manufacturers and retired soldiers formed commercial mine-clearance companies. Many were hopeful that the sort of major clearance contracts available in Kuwait would be let in the developing world, but the market proved much more whimsical. One of the first contracts let by the UN in the developing world caused some controversy as it was awarded to Royal Ordnance and Mechem, both companies that had been involved in the design and manufacture of mines. *The Independent* on 6 June 1994 condemned the deal under the headline 'UN aid goes to landmine makers'. It was further noted that the UN's Demining

Expert had been employed by Royal Ordnance until the previous year.

Other commercial contracts have been awarded to a number of companies, including Minetech, Mechem, DSL, SGS and Ronco, but they have generally been employed on specific clearance projects of limited duration. Many of the newly formed commercial companies have struggled to win a single contract. Non-governmental organizations and the UN usually mount long-term programmes aimed at transferring demining skills to indigenous peoples and gradually phase out the expatriate staff, a much more attractive option to those funding mine clearance.

In addition to the practical response on the ground, the media took a special interest in the mine issue. In print or on film, mines provided all the elements of a great story, horrific injuries to innocent people, hidden dangers, heroic efforts to clear mines, spectacular explosions and a moral dimension to tweak Western guilt. Articles with titles such as 'The Invisible Enemy', 'One Leg, One Life at a Time', 'Seeds of Death' and 'The New Killing Fields' appeared in newspapers and magazines world-wide, journalism giving way to sensationalism. Public opinion was outraged, money for mine-related projects started to flow and many relief and development non-governmental organizations attempted to get their work associated with the issue even if they were doing little to alleviate it. Significantly, the moral outrage was harnessed by the International Campaign to Ban Landmines (ICBL).

International Law and the International Campaign to Ban Landmines

On 12 August 1949 the Geneva Conventions were updated to reflect the changes in the nature of warfare in the previous decade. Although mines during this period had become 'almost a new arm of warfare', no specific restriction was placed on their use, apart from the forbidding of prisoners of war from employment on mine-clearance duties.[13] From this it must be concluded that mines were considered an acceptable weapon and that their effects, particularly on civilian populations, were not excessive, inhumane nor indiscriminate. Although even in the post-war

133

period civilians were injured by mines, the majority of those laid had been reasonably well marked and recorded.

Largely in response to the advent of scatterable mine systems, the clumsily named UN *Convention on Prohibitions or Restrictions on the Use of Certain Conventional Weapons Which May be Deemed to be Excessively Injurious and to have Indiscriminate Effects* (or CCW) was drawn up in 1980. This stated that minefields should be marked and recorded specifically to protect civilians, that remotely-delivered mines could only be used against areas containing military objectives, and that minefields should be cleared at the end of hostilities.[14] Only forty-one states signed the agreement and it had two important shortcomings: it did not formally apply to internal conflicts – where most of the problems occurred – and there was no means of implementing it.

Humanitarian groups felt that the CCW did not adequately address the problem of the unique threat that mines posed to civilians and that no armed force in recent times had consistently and accurately recorded the location of minefields.[15] In 1980 there was limited evidence to support this stance but by the early 1990s it was clear that thousands of civilians were victims of mines that had been laid without reference to the CCW and it was contended that mines had been used specifically to target civilians. As a result of this evidence it was claimed that the use of mines was already technically illegal under international humanitarian law because they were indiscriminate, failed to balance military utility against human suffering and flouted laws relating to the protection of the environment.[16] Indeed, a 1977 addition (Protocol 1) to the 1949 Geneva Conventions specifically stated that indiscriminate attacks which struck military and civilians alike were forbidden.

At an ICRC-hosted meeting of military experts in 1994 many felt that 'mines were an indispensable defence weapon in time of war and their banning would be undesirable or impossible in practical terms, but that some action should be taken to reduce the risks posed to civilians.'[17] Other delegates argued that anti-personnel mines had no place in their arsenals but no quorum could be reached because military and humanitarian considerations were different for each country.[18] Delegates at the conference also drew attention to the fact that, while there was a strong case to be made against virtually undetectable anti-personnel mines, those with a high metal content, self-neutralizing or self-destruct mechanisms and command-detonated mines could be deployed in war without greatly endangering civilians. However, as pictures of amputees were published around the world, mine protagonists were marginalized and calls for a complete ban on all types of anti-personnel mine, without exception, gained popular support.

In October 1992 a coalition of six non-governmental organizations – MAG, Handicap International, Vietnam Veterans of America Foundation, Human Rights Watch, Medico International and Physicians for Human Rights – harnessed popular support, sponsoring the creation of the ICBL and appointing Jody Williams its co-ordinator. Using powerful images of dreadfully wounded civilians and calling attention to the (exaggerated) scale of the problem, the campaign rapidly galvanized public opinion and prompted a number of countries to restrict or prohibit the use of anti-personnel mines unilaterally. The US Senator Patrick Leahy backed a successful proposal to prohibit the export of mines from the United States, prompting similar legislation in France and Italy. The Netherlands, Belgium, Denmark, Canada and Norway went a stage further and renounced the use of anti-personnel mines by mid-1996.

In August 1997 the death of Diana, Princess of Wales helped to focus attention on the ICBL which she had supported by visiting minefields in Angola and Bosnia. The ICBL received a further boost in October of the same year when the Nobel Peace Prize was awarded jointly to the campaign and Jody Williams. Riding on a wave of popular opinion, in December 1997 an international treaty to ban anti-personnel landmines was signed by 121 nations in Ottawa.

Although a triumph for popular will, about one-third of the UN's 185 member states, including the United States, China and Russia, the three largest military powers, did not sign the treaty. Other states such as Belize, Israel, Korea, India and Pakistan felt that a ban on such weapons would compromise their national security to an unacceptable degree. Even Egypt, Finland, Libya and Kuwait, all countries which had suffered the enduring consequences of millions of mines buried within their borders, declined to sign. Presumably they believed that the humanitarian dimension lay in protecting their people from aggressors rather than from the residual effect that mines may have. In an attempt to impose its politically-correct views on countries with a different perspective on national security, Britain threatened to withhold foreign aid to non-signatories.

The ICBL had laudable aims and was armed with an unassailable moral argument, but it was not without its critics. The treaty that had been agreed to represented to some mere parchment pacification, encouraging a false sense of security and not reducing the casualties caused by mines by a single leg.[19] Outlawing mines to others meant outlawing a legitimate means of defence in desperate situations. Muslims in the encircled Bosnian enclaves manufactured their own mines as one of their few means of preventing attacks from their aggressive neighbours. Many individuals working in mine clearance felt that the ICBL represented something of a double-edged sword. Certainly the campaign had brought a great deal of publicity to the issue, but it had distorted the size and the shape of the problem and distracted attention from the crux of the issue – the clearance of redundant minefields – making a moral issue out of a practical problem.[20]

Humanitarian Mine Clearance

The practical problems of mine clearance in the 1990s are perhaps greater than those of the 1940s. For the most part, mines in the Second World War were laid to a recorded, recognizable format and were found along the tide lines of the ebb and flow of battle. In the developing world, conflicts had no distinguishable front lines and the term minefield often suggested a formality that did not exist. Mine clearance has frequently been likened to finding a needle in a haystack, but in Cambodia, for example, finding the haystack was a problem in itself.

Locating minefields demands a sleuth-like approach as official records were rarely kept by developing world armies. More useful sources of information are the provincial hospitals where mine victims receive treatment. Admissions registers often indicate basic data such as types of injury and the patients' home villages, from which a rough idea of the mine situation may be gained. Oral surveys in mine victims' villages usually provide the best information since people who remained in those areas during the war often had a reasonable idea of where mines were laid. Physical evidence of minefields is usually quite subtle. As mined land is not productive, it is reclaimed by nature and in sub-tropical regions may be covered with dense vegetation. Craters or the bleached bones of animal victims may be apparent on detailed inspection, but the mines themselves are rarely seen as they are either buried or covered with vegetation. Attempting to establish the military history of the area and the position of defensive works may yield some clues, but in general an overgrown area and oral testimony are the only indication that the 'haystack' has been located.

Manual Clearance

The clearing of minefields is a slow and painstaking process and the intrinsic problem of reliably locating buried mines in a variety of soil conditions has defied easy solution. Electronic metal detectors have improved in performance greatly in recent years and are the main tool of the deminer. The wooden-cased PMD 6 or *Schumine* with its small, metal fuse was virtually undetectable with a 1940s detector but could be located at a range of over 30cm by the use of modern equipment such as the Ebinger 420. Some modern mines contain little or no metal and can only be reliably detected by prodding; but, fortunately, the majority of mines in the developing world are of Soviet origin and have sufficient metal content to make their detection relatively straightforward.

Mine clearance is a labour-intensive process. Deminers are organized into teams of between twenty and forty. (Nearly all deminers are male but MAG formed an effective women's team of deminers in Cambodia.) A team is split into pairs of deminers with each pair alternately working and resting throughout the day. A minefield is divided into a series of parallel lanes about 25m apart, sufficient to reduce the chance of multiple casualties in the event of an accident. One man from each pair works in a metre-wide lane for up to thirty minutes and then changes places with his partner who waits in a rest area behind the minefield. In the lane the deminer follows a repetitive drill: first he observes for trip wires, then he slowly swings the detector across the ground to his front, any vegetation is then carefully cut at ground level and the process is repeated. If the detector gives a warning, the area around the reading is carefully probed for evidence of a mine. Most mined areas contain metal fragments from shrapnel, wire or domestic items and less than 1 per cent of all detector alarms indicate the presence of a mine. If a mine is located, it is excavated sufficiently to place a small explosive charge alongside it and then detonated remotely. The process is mind-numbingly tedious, requiring considerable patience and rigid adherence to the drills.

In developing countries, which typically have very high rates of unemployment, demobilized soldiers are recruited by non-governmental organizations and the UN to clear minefields under expatriate supervision. Local deminers receive a monthly wage of around $100 and there is no shortage of volunteers despite the dangers of the work and the basic conditions in which they live. Inevitably accidents do occur, but, suprisingly, most mine clearance agencies report more casualties from road accidents than explosive accidents. The use of manual deminers in the developing world is more appropriate and effective than Western high technology – even if it were capable of producing comparable clearance rates.

Rates of clearance vary tremendously depending on the level of metal contamination, amount of vegetation, type of mine and the texture of the soil. It may be recalled that clearance rates in the Netherlands in 1945 were between 8,800 and 27,400sq.m per man per week. In the difficult conditions of the developing world clearance rates are frequently below 500sq. m per man per week.

In areas where there is gross metal contamination, soil with a high iron content or non-metallic mines detectors are useless and the clearance technique descends to a further level of tedium. Prodders may be used but the process is inexact. If searching for mines with a width of 5cm, the prodder must be inserted into the ground at an angle of 30 degrees at intervals of 3cm across the lane. To ensure adequate coverage along the lane the process must be repeated every 6cm, requiring a total of over 500 prodder insertions for every square metre. A more thorough and often more rapid method than prodding is excavating. With this technique an entrenching tool is used to cut soil to a depth of up to 30cm from the width of a lane in a sideways sweeping motion. Mines are stuck by the tool on their sides but as the pressure plate is on the top they do not detonate.

The HALO Trust in Mozambique operates one of the best excavation demining programmes. Many of the roads in Zambezia Province are closed owing to the suspicion that mines have been laid on them. Often the roads are tens of kilometres long and might contain one or two anti-tank mines. HALO staff train groups of villagers in the excavation technique and supervise them in clearing roads. Each villager excavates 100sq. m per day, and by using large teams roads are cleared thoroughly and relatively rapidly. As the villagers are paid for their efforts, money also gets pumped into the impoverished local economy.

The removing of vegetation is a time-consuming aspect of mine clearance and successful attempts have been made to undertake this process mechanically, most notably by MGM in Angola. They used a vegetation mulcher on a rotating hydraulic boom attached to a Namibian 'Wolf' mine-protected vehicle (closely related to those developed in Rhodesia) to grind up vegetation, greatly speeding up the process of manual clearance. Using this machine and a small team of deminers they were able to clear 64 km of overgrown road in thirty-four days in Bengo Province during 1996.

Dogs

Explosive-sniffer dogs play a relatively minor role in humanitarian mine clearance operations. They are useful for locating individual items, tracing the edges of minefields or for confirming that areas are clear but they are unable to work inside heavily mined areas as their olfactory senses get confused by multiple 'readings'. While they are able to work quickly in some areas, their work rate drops dramatically in hot and windy conditions and in areas of thick vegetation. At best they can work only four hours per day and they require extensive training and logistic support. Successful dog programmes have been operated by NPA in Mozambique since 1995, but because the dogs' role is limited and

139

their technique still not fully understood, most organizations prefer to stick to the more versatile methods of manual clearance.

MEDDS

In an effort to utilize the remarkable olfactory ability of dogs without the vagaries of the animal itself, the South African firm Mechem developed the MEDDS (Mechem Explosive and Drug Detection System) in the 1980s. The system was designed to locate isolated mines on roads and features a vapour-collecting system mounted on a mine-protected vehicle. Filters on the vapour-collecting mechanism are changed every 200m and then sent to a laboratory where they are checked by dogs. If a dog indicates that a filter is contaminated, the area from which it was taken is searched with detectors or free-running dogs. If the vehicle hits a mine while collecting samples its occupants remain unhurt and the vehicle can be quickly repaired. The system was used to help in clearing 2,000km of power-line service road in Mozambique during 1995/96.

Mechanical Clearance

As discussed in previous chapters, attempts have been made since 1919 to produce mine-clearance machines with mixed, but never wholly satisfactory results. Some machines are useful for breaching a single lane through a minefield in battle, but achieving close to the 100 per cent rates demanded of humanitarian mine clearance has proved elusive. Ploughs which proved effective at breaching Iraqi minefields in the Gulf War merely push mines aside and bury them under piles of earth. In 1992 the United Nations in Cambodia vainly attempted to use ploughs for clearance, but after much experimentation quite predictably found them inadequate. Rollers, the favoured Warsaw Pact breaching technique, are at best 80 per cent effective because they cannot respond to delicate contouring adequately and they do not always detonate mines in sun-baked soil. There have been some successes with flails but certain mine and soil types limit their use. However, NPA in Angola have used Scottish-built Aardvark flails to find the edges of minefields before their manual clearance.

The most promising recent innovations have been earth tillers such as those made by Krohn of Germany. These machines feature a spinning horizontal beam with tungsten teeth mounted on an armoured bulldozer. The toothed beam tills the soil to a depth of 40cm, detonating or disrupting mines as it moves forward. In May 1996 the machine was tested in Mozambique using 264 live mines, but the results were disappointing with 38 of them remaining undetonated and only partially disrupted after repeated passes by the machine. It was eventually allowed to conduct live clearance operations in Mozambique but with deminers following in its wake to locate the remaining mines and Krohn was continually plagued with problems.

Conclusion

In the closing years of the second millennium man is capable of exploring space but the technology for clearing minefields remains frustratingly primitive. There is a striking difference between the ease with which mines can be laid and the difficulty and the time it takes to clear them. The Pentagon's mine-clearance expert noted that, 'There is no single device ideally suited for demining that will become available in the foreseeable future; what is most apparent is that there are no easy solutions. Manual demining remains the primary means of demining former war zones.' Quite simply, there is no 'silver bullet' on the horizon. The diverse range of ground conditions and the variety of mines with their explosive force and sensitive fuzing mechanisms make the design criteria for mechanical clearance impossibly difficult to achieve. Despite the tedium and hazards of manual clearance, it remains the most flexible and effective technique.

References and Notes

1. In recognition of the fact that poorly-trained soldiers would use mines, nearly all were fitted with safe-to-arm mechanisms, which allowed five or ten minutes for the soldier to withdraw before the mine became active.

2. A notable exception was in Maputo Province, Mozambique, where extensive fences were erected around many mined villages; a fence around the Moamba minefield ran for over 40km and was up to 2m high.
3. Davies and Dunlop, p. 15.
4. Roberts and Williams, p. 216.
5. Davies and Dunlop, p. 19.
6. Sheehan and Croll, p. 11.
7. Roberts and Williams, p. 278.
8. Davies and Dunlop; ICRC, *Landmines: a Perverse Use of Technology*; Phillip C. Winslow, *Sowing the Dragon's Teeth* (Boston, MA: Beacon Press, 1997); Roberts and Williams; Arms Project of Human Rights Watch.
9. ICRC, *Landmines: Time for Action*, p. 8.
10. Roberts and Williams, p. 59.
11. Ibid., p. 141.
12. See Furedi, pp. 20–6 for discussion of this theme.
13. De Mulinen, p. 158.
14. Ibid., pp. 202–3.
15. Arms Project of Human Rights Watch, pp. 262–4.
16. Roberts and Williams, p. 489.
17. ICRC, *Landmines: Time for Action*, p. 33
18. Smith in *Brassey's Defence Yearbook 1996*, pp. 273–4.
19. G.F.Will, *Newsweek*, 21 July 1997, p. 80.
20. P. Jefferson, *Guardian*, 19 September 1997; J. Heilbrunn, *New Republic*, 13 October 1997.

Chapter 8

The Future

Technological, economic and social factors combine to ensure that not only will mines be used in the future, but that they will be used in increasing numbers. Future battles will be fought at high speed over large areas by relatively few men. The ability of mines rapidly to deny land and destroy the enemy with limited manpower in a cost-effective manner will be critical to defensive success. Indeed, the role of the mine will be expanded to such an extent that its original form will be scarcely recognizable. No longer will the victim have to activate the mine physically; the mine will sense its target at considerable range – tank, helicopter, possibly even jet aircraft and satellite – and deploy a lethal warhead.

Technology

Technology is an immensely powerful influence on the development of weapons and warfare. Modern electronics, computerization, digitization and sensing techniques can be incorporated into mines, greatly increasing both their effectiveness and their efficiency. The technical restraints on mines of the future will be limited only by man's 'devilish ingenuity', which, based on past experience, is considerable. The accelerating pace of technology creates a system whereby weapons are outdated before they are in service, thus speeding the process further. High-technology mines of the future will therefore be developed and

143

fielded only by major powers, providing flexible security for wealthy nations.

In recent years we have seen technology moving towards the intelligent minefield. The Swedish FFV 028 anti-tank system, introduced in the early 1980s, is capable of self-neutralizing at preset periods. Around the same time jet aircraft became capable of delivering scatterable systems such as the Gator, providing a deep-strike interdiction capability, an hitherto unknown aspect of mine warfare. In the late 1980s another new concept was introduced in the form of the American XM133 'minefield in a suitcase'. Featuring a container with seventeen anti-tank and four anti-personnel mines, the XM133 may be placed on the battle-field and activated by radio control, dispersing its mines when needed to a range of 35m. Each mine has an automatic self-destruct mechanism and it can also be destroyed by the radio control unit if necessary. The current range of mines under development in the United States blurs the distinction between mines and automated weapons systems. The XM93 wide-area mine uses seismic and acoustic detectors to identify enemy vehicles and launches a lethal warhead within a 360 degrees, 100m radius. The warhead is propelled vertically, identifies a target and then ignites a second propelling charge to fire itself through the top of a tank. The XM93 is also able to discriminate between enemy and friendly tanks, thus providing the unique ability of avoiding the 'own goals' so common in the past.

With increasing sophistication, fewer individual mines are required to cover the same ground. In the 1940s 2,000 anti-tank mines were needed per mile of front, by the 1970s the figure was 1,000, by 1980 it was 500, and today only twenty mines are required to cover the same mile. Twenty years from now perhaps only a single, highly sophisticated mine with multiple warheads will cover three or four miles. Taking the intelligent mine concept a stage further, wide-area mines with attacking ranges of several miles could be delivered by pilotless aircraft to enemy rear formations, providing an automated attack capability and destroying entire armoured formations. Intelligent mines will increase the vulnerability of tanks and hasten the decline of their

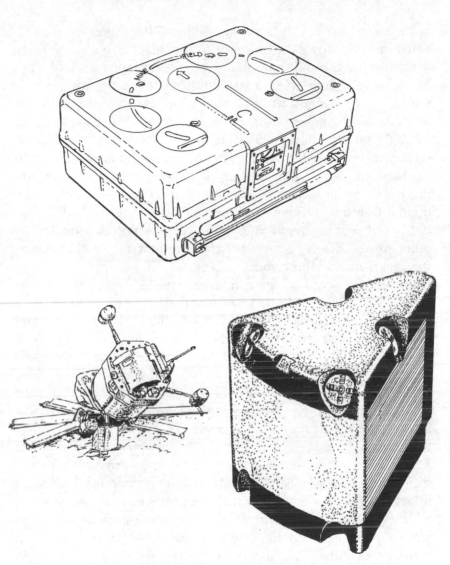

Modern American mines.
Top – XM 133 'minefield in a suitcase', bottom left – XM93 wide area mine and bottom right – ADAM, Area Denial Artillery Munition.

utility in favour of helicopter-borne forces. This will inevitably give rise to the proliferation of the anti-helicopter mine.

Since the 1960s there has been a steady increase in the number of military helicopters, initially for reconnaissance and logistic support, then as troop carriers and finally as attack and anti-armour platforms. The Vietcong used anti-helicopter mines activated by the down pressure of rotor blades; but they were dependent on the ability to predict where helicopters would land. Modern technology with radar and acoustic sensors will provide the ability to create anti-helicopter mines capable of identifying and attacking a helicopter travelling at speed. It is expected that by 2005 more than a million anti-helicopter mines could be in service throughout the world.[1] Initially these mines are likely to be hand-emplaced, but air- or artillery-delivered systems are inevitable in the future. The anti-helicopter mine is likely to be limited in range, forcing enemy helicopters to fly at higher altitudes and making them vulnerable to anti-aircraft missiles. In other words, it will perform the classical function of channelling the enemy into a killing zone.

For the foreseeable future, infantry will be a significant force on the battlefield since they remain the best means of holding ground. The increased vulnerability of vehicles from the air and from the next generation of mines will mean that infantry will continue to play a role even in the most technically advanced armies. Where the infantry are so too will there be a need for anti-personnel mines. While the presence of people can be detected by many types of sensor,[2] incorporating these devices into anti-personnel mines is extremely difficult owing to the range of stimuli that can activate them. For example, several types of sensor are incorporated into car- and home-security systems, but their false alarm rate is irritatingly high. It is therefore likely that mines such as the US artillery-delivered M86 fragmentation mine, which dispenses seven trip wires on landing and self-destructs after a predetermined time, will remain state of the art for a considerable time. The impact of the international campaign to ban landmines on the future of anti-personnel mines will be discussed later in this chapter.

Economics

Money has always been the most critical resource for waging war or maintaining defences. In this period of declining defence budgets and consequently declining military manpower, military planners are aware that future wars will have to be fought by the standing army since there will be no time in which to train reinforcements. Given that a major conflict in the future is likely to be fought over a large area, manpower will be spread perilously thinly. Economies in manpower can be compensated for by employing large numbers of mines. Using systems such as scatterable mines or the XM93, economies may be made in handling effort, transport resources, laying time and, of course, clearance resources. Furthermore, an intelligent mine that can attack its target reduces the amount of direct fire weaponry required and saves the time and effort required to move troops around to block enemy advances. As mines contribute economically to the defensive, so they also contribute to offensive strength by releasing forces to strengthen the mobile reserve.[3]

Social Factors

The Western, urban-bred soldier is unable to withstand the hardships of living in the field as even his recent predecessors did, and it is unlikely that he will be able to withstand long periods under the most demanding combat conditions.[4] Disturbing images of war being beamed live into the homes of a Western society unwilling to witness suffering, the requirement for minimal friendly casualties, and the need for troops fighting on foreign soil to return home as soon as possible, create a strong demand for the automation of military equipment. The intelligent mine is therefore perhaps the 'perfect soldier': it does not sleep, require feeding or paying and is unable to feel pain. The mine, the silent sentinel, may become the war hero of the twenty-first century.

Developing Countries

While mines may in future come to be regarded with greater approval in wealthy countries, in the developing world they are likely to continue to be seen as a scourge. Developing countries unable to afford intelligent mines will continue to use conventional blast mines from the bargain basement of the arms bazaar.

The use of off-route mines by guerrilla groups may become more important as principal roads become sealed, but, in general, the situation is likely to remain largely unchanged. Most of the wars on the fault line of Communism have burnt out and the next wars will be fought along ethnic and tribal lines. As the cheapest mines on the market are those manufactured in the former Warsaw Pact countries, their mines are likely to continue in widespread use. The style of mine laying will more closely resemble that in the Former Yugoslavia where minefields were laid around mono-ethnic areas in a reasonably predictable format.

Countermeasures

Counter-mine technology in the future will be of increasing importance. The broader range and the greater number of mines on the fast moving battlefield will mean that all units, including those in the rear, will require several types of countermeasure. In a period in which a ceiling is placed on maximum casualty levels, more will have to be done to prevent troops from being injured by mines and the market for mine-protected vehicles will expand.

Countering mines will continue to be enormously difficult and no technology exists that can adequately handle all mine scenarios. Improved rollers, ploughs and flails are being developed but each technique has its limitations. The earth tiller offers no distinct advantage in combat situations over other mechanical clearance methods, but it may have a place in peacetime clearance if the concept is combined with a complementary system. Fuel–air-explosive clearance methods will become more numerous and will offer a brute strength approach to breaching in selected combat scenarios.[5] With the arrival of the intelligent minefield will come the 'intelligent deminer' equipped with electronic countermeasures, deactivating and bypassing remote sensors and blocking radio signals. The deminer of the present may dream of working behind a computer in an air-conditioned cabin, but he is likely to remain very much on the ground for the immediate future.

Scatterable and intelligent mines pose an entirely new set of countermeasure conundrums. The first problem will be the reporting of their presence, as they will appear on the battlefield without warning. Once a report has been passed it will need to be disseminated instantly to avoid movement into the area. If countermeasures are available they will need to be deployed within hours and be capable of eliminating the threat extremely quickly. This could probably be achieved only by using sophisticated electronic countermeasures and the initiative, as always, will remain with the mine designer. The current generation of scatterable, anti-personnel mines can be countered using a type of vehicle-mounted plough and its use will mitigate, rather than neutralize the threat. Combat clearance by hand will be enormously difficult and, given the expected pace of future wars, may never be achieved rapidly enough.

Inevitably some self-destruct mechanisms will fail and mines embodying them will have to be cleared in peacetime. As modern mines are surface-laid, their detection by thermal imagers will be fairly simple and they have sufficient metal content in the form of shaped charge linings and electronic packages to be easily located with conventional detectors. With future mine development focused on sophisticated mines of high metal content, the evolution of conventional, minimal metal mines may be complete. Therefore the gap between mine detectabilty and detector capability should narrow as greater performance is achieved from metal detectors.

Since the early 1990s there has been considerable investment in counter-mine technology for both combat and peacetime operations. New approaches are divided into three broad categories: imaging sensors such as passive infra-red, active infra-red and ground-penetrating radar; substance analysers such as improved metal detectors and explosive vapour detectors; and a combination of two or more different types of sensor in a single piece of equipment.

An airborne active infra-red system is under development in the United States which is capable of detecting thermal differences in the patterns in the earth caused by minefields.[6] The interpretation of data from this system will need to be refined considerably before it is suitable for peacetime operations. Attempts are also being made to develop ground-penetrating radar for airborne use and a combination of the two technologies may yield promising results.[7] For combat situations the sensors will be carried on pilotless aircraft and relayed via sophisticated command, control and information systems to troops on the battlefield who will be able to orientate themselves to the minefield by satellite-fed, ground-positioning systems. Speed of detection and passage of information will be of critical importance on the high-speed battlefield if maximum benefit is to be gained from these systems.

Vehicle and hand-held counter-mine systems will also incorporate the new technology. Indeed, the use of airborne infra-red systems is a result of the Gulf War experience, when tank crews reported that at times they could distinguish mines through their thermal imaging sights.[8] Bio-sensors, artificial olfactory systems, are under development which could provide the capability to detect explosive vapours in real time (as opposed to the retrospective Mechem Explosive and Drug Detection System or MEDDS) and may provide a useful tool for route clearance or the tracing of the edges of minefields.

In the medium to long term a combination of different types of sensor may provide the key to more rapid peacetime clearance operations. For example, a bio-sensor may provide a general indication of the presence of a mine as explosive vapours are detected at a radius of over 5m from the source, and a metal detector could pinpoint the mine itself. Alternatively, a metal detector and a small ground-probing radar could be combined and only alarms from both systems would need to be investigated by a deminer, greatly increasing the speed of clearance. Attempts are being made in several countries to combine sensors on remotely-controlled vehicles,[9] but these systems will not be suitable for use in dense minefields or difficult terrain. For the foreseeable future, the peacetime clearance of 'dumb' mines will continue to be undertaken by deminers on foot using metal detectors and prodders, although the adding of additional sensing systems will improve both the speed and the safety of their work.

Impact of the International Campaign to Ban Landmines

As a result of the campaign (ICBL) there is now a widespread revulsion in the West at the indiscriminate effects of anti-personnel mines. However, the effects of the campaign are unlikely to be beneficial. As mentioned in the previous chapter, only 121 of the 185 members of the United Nations have so far (early 1998) signed the ban treaty. The pro- and the anti-countries being divided into those which consider hostilities possible in the future and those that feel secure.

Given that anti-tank and anti-helicopter mines will be fielded by all countries in the future and that anti-personnel mines will continue to be deployed by potentially warring nations, the impact of the ban will be minimal. Even countries which sign the treaty *in extremis* may look after their national security interests before honouring the voluntary treaty. If the truth is the first casualty of war, then the law must surely be the second. Countries that use anti-personnel mines may be stigmatized in popular opinion, but in war the opinion of outsiders counts for little.

Restrictions placed on the exporting of mines may even have a damaging effect. As mines cannot be obtained through official channels, then black marketing will occur or nations may establish their own production facilities. Nations such as the United States will not be able to sell their intelligent mines, thus increasing the unit price and forcing other countries wishing to field similar systems to develop their own at great cost.

Humanitarian mine clearance will also be affected by the huge amount of publicity generated by the ban campaign. As the estimates of the total number of mines have been grossly inflated, there will be considerable concern when clearance programmes have removed all known mined ground and the final tally of mines represents only a fraction of those thought to have been laid. Furthermore, because the West is willing to provide clearance resources after a conflict, host countries will have no incentive to initiate any such operations themselves. There have already been instances in Africa and the Balkans where officials have stalled Western-backed initiatives in an attempt to obtain a financial 'lubricant' to ease the passage of official protocols.

While the future effects of the ICBL in practical terms will be extremely limited, the campaign is ultimately heartening. Armies will be more prudent when employing mines and the well-publicized difficulties of clearance may result in improvements in the marking and the recording of minefields. The most important effect of the ICBL is that it mobilized public opinion and brought the horrors of war to the public. John Keegan wrote that 'culture determines the nature of war';[10] if that is so, then the society which allowed the mine to proliferate and is now repelled by it may be close to rejecting the notion of war itself. The triumph of the Western way of war may eventually lead to the triumph of the Western way of peace, once history has unravelled itself and nation states fit neatly inside their natural borders.

Conclusions

Irrespective of the ICBL, 'it is inconceivable that any modern army could operate effectively in a high intensity conflict without recourse to a very large number of mines of all types.'[11] Mine and counter-mine technology will become increasingly important on the battlefield as armies try to move faster, over larger areas and with less manpower. The impact of mines on civilians will have to be considered carefully by armies wishing to maintain the moral high ground. However, by providing reliable, self-destruct mechanisms, technology will help to avert the insidious, long-term effects of mines that international treaties cannot. Poor countries will continue to use dumb mines to defend against their aggressors and they will still be used by guerrilla groups who abide by their own moral code. New, Western-sponsored clearance technology will eventually help to mitigate their worst effects in the post-war period, and it may be hoped that a humanitarian crisis of the current proportions may be avoided. After 2,500 years the evolution of the victim-operated trap is not complete, the 'infernal machine' is here to stay.

References and Notes

1. Heyman, p. 60.
2. During the 1980s the Soviets produced the VP13 seismic control system for use with fragmentation mines; it saw service in Afghanistan in small numbers but is not believed to have been employed elsewhere.
3. Sloan, p. 113.
4. Heyman, p. 58.
5. Gander, Hewish and Ness, pp. 47–52.
6. *Jane's Defence Weekly*, 14 February 1995, p. 21.
7. Hewish and Ness.
8. Schneck, p. 4.
9. Hewish and Ness.
10. Keegan, p. 387.
11. Heyman, p. 7.

Bibliography

Books

Ambrose, Stephen E., *D-Day June 6, 1944: The Climactic Battle of World War II* (New York: Simon & Schuster, 1994)

The Arms Project of Human Rights Watch, *Landmines: A Deadly Legacy* (New York: HRW and PHR, 1993)

Atkinson, Rick, *Crusade* (London: HarperCollins, 1994)

Beck, Alfred M. *et al.*, *The US Army in World War 2, The Technical Services: The Corps of Engineers: The War against Germany* (Washington, DC: Center for Military History, 1985)

Belote, James H. and William M. Belote, *Corregidor: The Saga of a Fortress* (New York: Harper & Row, 1967)

Bishop, M.C. and J.C.N. Coulston, *Roman Military Equipment* (London: Batsford, 1993)

Brassey's Defence Yearbook 1996 (London: Brassey's, 1996)

Caesar, *The Conquest of Gaul*, trans. S.A. Handford (Harmondsworth: Penguin, 1951)

Carey, Peter (ed.), *The Faber Book of Reportage* (London: Faber, 1987)

Coll, B.D., J.E. Keith and H.H. Rosenthal, *The US Army in World War 2, The Technical Services: The Corps of Engineers: Troops and Equipment* (Washington, DC: Department of the Army, 1968)

Cordesman, Anthony H. and Abraham R. Wagner, *The Lessons of Modern Warfare:*
Vol.1, *The Arab–Israeli Conflicts 1973–89* (Boulder, CO: Westview, 1990)
——, *The Lessons of Modern Warfare*, Vol.4, *The Gulf War* (Boulder, CO: Westview, 1996)

Cruttwell, C.R.M.F., *A History of the Great War 1914–1918* (Oxford: Clarendon Press, 1934)

Davis, R.H.C., *The Medieval Warhorse: Origin, Development and Redevelopment* (London: Thames & Hudson, 1989)

Davies, Paul and Nick Dunlop, *War of the Mines: Cambodia and the Impoverishment of a Nation* (London: Pluto Press, 1994)

Dixon, Aubrey C. and Otto Heilbrunn, *Communist Guerrilla Warfare* (London: Allen & Unwin, 1954)

Doubler, Michael D., *Closing with the Enemy: How GIs Fought the War in Europe 1944–1945* (Lawrence, KS: University Press of Kansas, 1994)

Edmonds, Brig.-Gen. Sir James E. and Lt-Col. R. Maxwell Hyslop, *The History of the Great War: Military Operations in France and Belgium 1918*, Vol.I and V.

Engineer Agency for Resource Inventories, *Landmine and Countermine Warfare:* Vol.3, *North Africa, 1940–43*; Vol.4, *Italy, 1943–44*; Vol.5, *Korea, 1950–54*; Vol.9, *Vietnam, 1964–69*; Vol.16, *Western Europe*; Vol.18, *Eastern Europe* (Washington, DC: June 1972)

Farwell, Byron, *The Great War in Africa* (London: Norton, 1986)

Ffoulkes, C., *Arms and Armament: A Historical Survey of Weapons of the British Army* (London: Harrap, 1945)

Foertsch, Herman, *The Art of Modern Warfare* (New York: Oskar Piest, 1940)

Frost, Frank, *Australia's War in Vietnam* (Sydney: Allen & Unwin, 1987)

Furedi, Frank, *The Culture of Fear: Risk Taking and the Morality of Low Expectation* (London: Cassell, 1997)

Gander, T.J. and Peter Chamberlain, *Weapons of the Third Reich: An Encyclopaedic Survey of Small Arms, Artillery and Special Weapons of the German Land Forces 1939–45* (Garden City, NY: Doubleday, 1979)

Gardner, Brian, *The German East* (London: Cassell, 1963)

Gilbert, Felix, *Hitler Directs His War: the Secret Records of His Daily Military Conferences* (New York: Oxford University Press, 1950)

Gillingham, John, *The Wars of the Roses* (Baton Rouge, LA: Louisiana State University Press, 1981)

Hamilton, Nigel, *Monty: The Making of a General 1887–1942* (London, McGraw-Hill, 1981)

Hartcup, Guy, *The Challenge of War: Britain's Scientific and Engineering Contributions to World War Two* (New York: Taplinger, 1970)

Hay, Lt-Gen. John H., *Vietnam Studies: Tactical and Material Innovations* (Washington, DC: Department of the Army, 1974)

Heyman, Maj. Charles, *Trends in Landmine Warfare* (Coulsdon: Jane's Information Group, 1995)

Hogben, Maj. Arthur, *Designed to Kill* (Wellingborough: Patrick Stephens, 1987)

Hoppen, Alison, *The Fortification of Malta by the Order of St. John* (Edinburgh: Scottish Academic Press, 1979)

Hoyt, Edwin P., *The GI's War: The Story of American Soldiers in Europe in World War 2* (New York: McGraw-Hill, 1988)

James, Peter and Nick Thorpe, *Ancient Inventions* (New York: Ballantine, 1994)

Jefferson, Paul, *Warsaw Pact Mines* (Basildon: Miltra Engineering, 1992)

Keegan, John, *A History of Warfare* (New York: Vintage Books, 1993)

Knight, Ian, *Brave Men's Blood: The Epic of the Zulu War 1879* (Guild Publishing, 1990)

Liddell Hart, B.H. (ed.), *The Rommel Papers* (London: Cassell, 1953)

——, *The Red Army* (New York: Harcourt Brace, 1956)

——, *The Tanks*, Vol.2 (London: Cassell, 1959)

McCartney, Eugene S., *Warfare by Land and Sea* (Boston, MA: Marshall Jones, 1923)

McDonald, Charles B., *The US Army in World War 2, European Theater of Operations: The Siegfried Line Campaign* (Washington, DC: Department of the Army, 1963)

McKenzie, W.M., *The Battle of Bannockburn: A Study in Medieval Warfare* (Stevenage: Strong Oak Press, 1989, first published 1913)

McLaughlin-Green, Constance, Harry C. Thompson and Peter C. Roots, *The US Army in World War 2: The Technical Services: The Ordnance Department: Planning Munitions for War* (Washington, DC: Office of the Chief of Military History, Department of the Army, 1955)

Majdalany, Fred, *The Fall of Fortress Europe* (New York: Doubleday, 1968)

——, *The Battle of El Alamein* (London: Weidenfeld & Nicolson, 1965)

Mayo, Linda, *The US Army in World War 2, The Technical Services: The Ordnance Department on Beachhead and Battlefront* (Washington, DC: Office of the Chief of Military History, 1968)

Montross, L., *War through the Ages* (New York: Harpers, 1944)

Nef, John U., *War and Human Progess* (New York: Norton, 1950)

Orpen, Neil and H.J. Martin, *Salute to the Sappers*, 2 vols (Johannesburg: Sappers Association, 1981)

Pakenham-Walsh, Maj.-Gen. R.P., *The History of the Corps of Royal Engineers*, Vols VIII and X (Chatham: Institute of Royal Engineers, 1958 and 1986)

Perry, Milton F., *Infernal Machines: The Story of Confederate Submarine and Mine Warfare* (Baton Rouge, LA: Louisiana State University Press, 1985; first published, 1965)

Raschen, Dan, *Send Port and Pyjamas* (London: Buckland Publications, 1987)

Roberts, Shawn and Jody Williams, *After the Guns Fall Silent: The Enduring Legacy of Landmines* (Washington, DC: Vietnam Veterans of America Foundation, 1995)

Sloan, Lt-Col. C.E.E., *Mine Warfare on Land* (London: Brassey's, 1986)

Southern, P. and K.Dixon, *The Late Roman Army* (London: Batsford, 1996)

Starry, Donn A., *Mounted Combat in Vietnam* (Washington, DC: Department of the Army, 1977)

Stiff, Peter, *Taming the Landmine* (Alberton, RSA: Galago, 1986)

Trump, D.H., *Malta: An Archaeological Guide* (Valetta: Progress Press, 1972)

US Department of State, *Hidden Killers: The Global Landmine Crisis* (Washington, DC: Bureau of Political-Military Affairs, Publication 10225, 1994)

Veasy-Fitzgerald, Brian, *The Book of the Dog* (Los Angeles, CA: Bordon, 1948)

Voldman, Daniele, *Attention Mines 1944–47* (Paris: France-Empire, 1985) [trans, A. Willis]

Webster, Donovan, *Aftermath: The Remnants of War* (New York: Pantheon Books, 1996)

Westing, Arthur H., *Explosive Remnants of War* (London: Taylor & Francis, for SIPRI, 1985)

Westover, John G., *Combat Support in Korea* (Washington, DC: Center of Military History, 1955; reprinted 1984)

Wood, Maj.-Gen. Sir Elliot, *Life and Adventure in Peace and War* (London: Edward Arnold, 1924)

Articles

'Notes on Submarine Mines Commonly Called Torpedoes', *Professional Papers of the Corps of Royal Engineers*, Vol.15, 1866

'Correspondence', *Royal Engineers Journal*, Vol.14, No.169, 1884

'Events', *idem*, Vol.16, No.182, 1886

'Defence of Ladysmith', *idem*, Vol.33, No.395, 1903

Beckingham, Capt H.W., 'Minefield Clearance in Guernsey', *Royal Engineers Journal*, Vol.107, No.2, August 1993

Buttery, Capt P.A., 'Minefield Clearance in Central Bosnia', *Royal Engineers Journal*, Vol.108, No.3, December 1994

Crothswait, Maj. M.L., 'Demolitions and Minelaying: Some German Methods', *Royal Engineers Journal*, Vol.66, March–December 1952

Dewing, Capt R.H., 'Anti-tank Mines in Mobile Warfare', *Royal Engineers Journal*, March 1924

Fitzpatrick, Lt-Col. N.T., 'An Anti-tank Exercise (Southern Command, 1934)', *Royal Engineers Journal*, Vol.49, March–December 1935

Gander, T., M.Hewish and L.Ness, 'Disposing the Threat', *International Defense Review*, 10/1995

Golino, L. and A.Grimaldi, 'The Mined Obstacle in American Tactical Doctrine', *Defence Today*, April 1983

Halloran, B.F, 'Soviet Landmine Warfare', *Military Engineer*, Vol.64, No.418, March–April 1972

Hewish, M. and L.Ness, 'Mine Detection Technologies', *International Defense Review*, 10/1995

Hogben, Maj. A., 'Background Notes on the Butterfly Bomb Attacks', *Royal Engineers Journal*, Vol.107, No.2, August 1993

Hough, Capt R.H., 'Disposal of Old Minefields in the United Kingdom', *Royal Engineers Journal*, Vol.68, No.3, September 1954

Jane's Defence Weekly, 'Briefing: Defuzing the World's Landmine Threat', 14 February 1996

Lambert, Col. J.M., 'Tin Triangles', *Royal Engineers Journal*, Vol.66, March–December 1952

Moore, Brig. P.N.M., 'Mine Clearance – El Alamein', *Royal Engineers Journal*, Vol.106, No.3, December 1992

'Nitebar', 'Seventy Men: a Troop of Sappers with the 8th Army in Early 1943', *Royal Engineers Journal*, Vol.107, No.1, April 1993

Schneck, W., 'Desert Storm Countermine Improvisations', *Engineer*, July 1992

Sickler, R., 'The Engineer Challenge', *Engineer*, November 1992

Young, Brig. B.K., 'The Development of Landmine Warfare', *Army Quarterly*, Vol.49, No.2, January 1945

Manuals, Pamphlets and Reports

Assault Training and Development Centre, *Mine Clearance: Data on Devices*, 1944

Assistant Chief of the General Staff, *The Handbook of Land Service Ammunition*, Part 1: *General*, *Ch. 1: Historical* (Woolwich: Quality Assurance Directorate (Weapons), 1971)

Burleigh, Capt A.C., 'Foreign Material', unpublished notes in Aberdeen Ordnance Museum Library, Maryland

De Mulinen, Frederick, *Handbook on the Law of War for Armed Forces* (Geneva: ICRC, 1987)

Department of the Army, *Field Manual FM 5–31, Landmines and Booby Traps* (Washington, DC,1 November 1943)

——, *Field Manual: Landmine Warfare* (Washington, DC, 1949)

——, *Technical Manual TM 5.223D, British, French and Italian Mine-warfare Equipment* (Washington, DC, May 1952)

——, *Technical Manual TM5-223,4, Soviet Minewarfare Equipment* (Washington, DC, August 1954)

——, *Field Manual FM 20–32: Landmine Warfare* (Washington, DC, 1966)

——, *Army Ammunition Data Sheets for Landmines* (Washington, DC, February 1977)

——, *Field Manual FM 20–32: Mine/Countermine Operations* (Washington, DC, December 1985)

Donovan P.D. and R.D. Moat, *RARDE Memorandum 38/83, History of Mines in Land Warfare* (Fort Halstead, Kent, June 1983)

General Staff, *The Russo-Japanese War: Reports from Officers Attached to the Japanese Forces in the Field* (London: War Office, 1906)

——, *Hints on Reconnaissance for Mines and Landmines in the Area Evacuated by the Germans*, May 1917

HQ 2nd British Infantry Division, *Report on Operation TAPPET, Mine-clearance in 2 Division and 1 Belgian Corps Area 15 November 1946–28 July 1947*, BAOR, August 1947 (in Royal Engineers Library)

Instructions to RAF BD Units, various dates, 1939–46 (in Imperial War Museum)

International Committee of the Red Cross, *Anti-Personnel Landmines – Friend or Foe? A Study of the Military Use and Effectiveness of Anti-personnel Mines*, March 1966

——, *Protocols Additional to the Geneva Conventions of 12 August 1949*, 1977

——, *International Law Concerning the Conduct of Hostilities*, 1989

——, *Landmines: Time for Action: International Humanitarian Law*, n.d.

McBean, Wg Cmd J.A., *RE Bomb Disposal: Historical Notes 1948–78*, EODTIC, 1980 (in Royal Engineers Library)

Military Operational Research Unit, *Report No. 7, Minefield Clearance and Casualties*, 3 May 1946 (in Royal Engineers Library)

RARDEC (Christchurch), *Keeping You Going*, July 1990

Royal Engineers Planning Staff, *The Requirement for AT Mines in the Period 1965–75*, declassified, 1960

Royal School of Military Engineering, *Evaluation of Mine Detectors for Use in the Falkland Islands*, August 1982

School of Military Engineering, *The Work of the Royal Engineers in the European War 1914–19*, Chatham, SME, 1924

——, *Fortification Circular No.57, German Traps and Mines*, Chatham: SME, 1919

Sheehan, E. and M.Croll, *Landmine Casualties in Mozambique* (Maputo: HALO Trust, 1993)

War Department, *Field Manual FM 5–31, Landmines and Booby Traps* (Washington, DC, 1 November 1943)

——, *Report 860, Aerial Bombardment of Minefields* (Washington, DC, 30 August 1944)

——, *Technical Manual TM-E-30451, Handbook on German Military Forces* (Washington, DC, 1945)

War Office, *Military Engineering, Part 1, Field Defences* (Chatham: SME, 1902)
——, *Illustrated Record of German Army Equipment 1939–45*, Vol.V, *Mines, Mine Detectors and Demolition Equipment* (London, 1947)
——, *The Second World War 1939–45, Army: Military Engineering (Field)* (London, 1952)
Weekly Tank Notes, Vol.1, 10 August–2 November 1918; Vol.2, 9 November 1918–8 February 1919 (in Bovington Tank Museum)
Zatylkin, B.V., *The Occupation of Sapper* (Moscow, Dosaaf SSR, 1978; translated from Russian)

Other Periodicals and Newspapers Consulted
Armada
Defence
Harper's Weekly
Independent
International Defense Review
Jane's Defence Weekly
Newsweek
Scientific American
Sunday Telegraph
The New York Times
The Times (London)
Wall Street Journal

Index